It certainly has been a great privilege to work with Linda on this book. Drawn from her own experiences and keen observations, she offers an interesting approach to the journey of faith for anyone who is seeking the Lord's direction. *Triumphant Living* provides an avenue for the Holy Spirit to speak to the reader through the Word, in the context of life situations. While Linda's Assembly of God background did not lead us to agreement on how the Holy Spirit works, the way of salvation and the challenges of Christian living comes clearly across in the book.

Pastor Floyd Stolzenburg,
Emmanuel Lutheran Church, Columbus, Ohio

"I have known Linda Marcum but for a short time. I have found her, however, to be a genuine Christian woman. Her heart's desire is to please the Lord and help others with her gifts. The book, *Triumphant Living,* is both practical and insightful. This book is an opulent source for many people who desire to grow spiritually and be encouraged in their faith."

J. Phillip Epperson, D. Min.
Director, Prayer Across America, Oak forest, IL

Triumphant Living

Triumphant Living

Linda Kay Marcum

Tate Publishing & *Enterprises*

Triumphant Living
Copyright © 2007 by Linda Kay Marcum. All rights reserved.

This title is also available as a Tate Out Loud product. Visit www.tatepublishing.com for more information.

No part of this publication may be reproduced, stored in a retrieval system or transmitted in any way by any means, electronic, mechanical, photocopy, recording or otherwise without the prior permission of the author except as provided by USA copyright law.

Scripture quotations marked "NKJV" are taken from The New King James Version / Thomas Nelson Publishers, Nashville: Thomas Nelson Publishers. Copyright © 1982. Used by permission. All rights reserved.

This book is designed to provide accurate and authoritative information with regard to the subject matter covered. This information is given with the understanding that neither the author nor Tate Publishing, LLC is engaged in rendering legal, professional advice. Since the details of your situation are fact dependent, you should additionally seek the services of a competent professional.

The material on nutrition in chapter eight is only given as information and is not intended as medical advice. Please consult your physician before making any changes in your life.

The opinions expressed by the author are not necessarily those of Tate Publishing, LLC.

Published by Tate Publishing & Enterprises, LLC
127 E. Trade Center Terrace | Mustang, Oklahoma 73064 USA
1.888.361.9473 | www.tatepublishing.com

Tate Publishing is committed to excellence in the publishing industry. The company reflects the philosophy established by the founders, based on Psalms 68:11,
"The Lord gave the word and great was the company of those who published it."

Book design copyright © 2007 by Tate Publishing, LLC. All rights reserved.
Cover design by Janae J. Glass
Interior design by Elizabeth A. Mason

Published in the United States of America

ISBN: 978-1-6024755-3-3
07.05.05

This book is dedicated to my husband, Jim, with all my love, along with Brian, Kathy, Megan and Kirsten, my mother and father, Ralph and Latsy Harper, my brother Ed, and sister-in-law, Liliana. And to all those who are searching for God and those who want a deeper relationship with Him.

Acknowledgements

I had a keen sense that God was directing everything I did in writing *Triumphant Living*. As I worked, He was ready at every turn to supply what I needed, from the content, to a new computer, to help with this manuscript. Pastor Floyd Stolzenburg, from Emmanuel Lutheran Church in Columbus, Ohio, helped me tremendously. I appreciate his expertise in both Biblical knowledge and writing skills. In every chapter, he had me write and rewrite until at times, I was almost weary, but the end results proved to be worth the effort.

My own pastor, Gene Speich, helped me prepare the contents and encouraged me as I wrote. I'm also indebted to Jeanne Kemple, Robin Madosky Fay Hall, and Janet Norris who proof-read the manuscript. Also my friends, Adda Sutter and Cookie Eckels, listened and encouraged me as I discussed the contents of this book. Last but not least, I want to thank my husband, Jim, who has always stood by me in each endeavor I undertake. I appreciate his constant love and encouragement in all I do.

Contents

Foreword	13
Introduction	15
A Triumphant Life	17
Thy Word is a Lamp Unto my Feet	35
Twelve Keys to Effective Praying	47
The Glorious Church— The Bride of Christ	73
Builders in the Kingdom	99
Tools for the Builders	115
Spiritual Warfare—How to Battle the Devil and Win	129
My People Perish for Lack of Knowledge	151
A Royal Priesthood, A Chosen Generation	169
You Can't Take it With You— or Can You?	181

FOREWORD

Linda Kay Marcum's book is a fresh wind blowing across the Kingdom of God. She has the ship of her life firmly rooted in the word of God. Her Baptist roots are clearly seen in her commitment to Scripture. One day she hoisted the sail of her life into the breezes of the Holy Spirit. A dramatic encounter with the Spirit in 1997 changed her forever. She is now active in the Assembly of God.

Triumphant Living takes the reader on a journey to the very heart of the Holy! She affirms the greatness of God, the grace of God, the church of God, and the gifts of God! There is also instruction for spiritual battles and hope for the future. This book is dangerous to the Devil! This book will change your life.

Dr. Ron Phillips
Senior Pastor, Central Baptist Church of Hixon, Tennessee

INTRODUCTION

It was in the year 2000 or 2001 that the idea for this book came to me. I was listening to Dr. Laura on the radio. A caller had asked how he could find the right church, and how to develop a relationship with God. I thought how I would answer that caller. My thoughts became this book. I did no writing at that time, but the words and contents were formed in my mind.

After September 11, 2001, I began to write. I prayed, "Lord, what would you say to your people today? What are Your words for those who are seeking you in this generation?" I listened to what God spoke into my heart. Then I wrote it down. As I read and meditated on what I wrote, the Lord began to do a work in me. I was already living for the Lord; and I had a degree of intimacy with Him, but as a result of what the Lord spoke to me, my walk with Him grew even deeper. Writing this book has impacted my life on many levels. I've learned to obey and worship Him more.

If the Lord can change my life that much, I know He can do the same for anyone. As you read this book, I hope that the Holy Spirit works in your life as He did in mine. I hope that each reader is drawn into a greater intimacy with God.

A Triumphant Life

In the 19th century, George Mueller operated several orphanages in England. He had no money for their operation; every need was supplied by prayer. One morning one home had nothing for breakfast. Mueller prayed for food. Soon a knock came at the door. The driver of a milk truck had broken down in front of the orphanage, and he could not make his deliveries. He asked if Mueller could use the milk so that it would not be wasted. Not long afterwards, a baker knocked at the door and asked if they could use bread. This is but one example of how Mueller relied on God to meet all the needs of the orphanages. Every need Mueller had was met the same way—he prayed and God provided.

Now you might not run an orphanage and rely on God for all its necessities as Mueller did, but what if every time you had a need, you could pray and trust God to meet that need just as he did?

That would be great, but it would never happen to me. I'm just an ordinary person, not a super person.

Neither was George Mueller. He was an ordinary person just like you and me, but he had a relationship with an extraordinary God. The same God who answered Mueller's prayers wants to do the same for you. Everything that was available to Mueller is available to every Christian. You only need to know how to tap into God's resources. Each chapter of this book contains information that will help you on your journey. By the time you finish reading, you'll know how to have a relationship with Christ that is just as dynamic as George Mueller's.

The quality of your existence on earth depends upon which road of life you choose to travel. The majority of people choose the broad road. Jesus spoke of this when He said, "Wide is the gate and broad is the way that leads to destruction, and there are many who go in by it" (Matthew 7:13). The final destination of this road is eternal separation from God. The alterative is the narrow road that leads to everlasting life. "Narrow is the gate and difficult is the way which leads to life, and there are few who find it" (Matthew 7:14). In this chapter, we'll examine both highways to see the quality of life they bring and the end result of each.

Come with me as we start our journey on the world's broad highway. As we enter this thoroughfare, we find the path is well traveled. People are bumping into each other as they compete for recognition and power. All who trek this road generally love money and the things it can buy. Many have expensive cars, nice homes and big screen TV's. Whether they have little or a lot, they're occupied with thoughts of cash and how to get a little more of it. The main focus of their lives is acquiring more stuff. Jesus said, "Where your treasure is, there your heart will be also" (Matthew 6:21).

But wait! There's a steep curve up ahead that they didn't see coming. Suddenly, their blissful life-style comes to a crashing halt. This unexpected hurdle could have many causes—the loss of a job, a painful divorce or the death of a child. Suddenly, their life has fallen apart. This wasn't supposed to happen on the highway to success. They're devastated and groping in the darkness, but there's nothing to hold on to. Their money and nice home are no comfort in a time of crisis.

Eventually, they recover and continue on their journey. They're still on their pursuit of money and things, but as we exam their lives more closely we find that their existence seems empty. There's a longing that money can't buy. They try other things of the world, but all those pleasures are short-lived. That unexplained longing simply cannot be satisfied.

Years pass and suddenly they've reached the end of their destination. Their life is over, and now perhaps they'll find peace. Or so they think. A few seconds after they die, they realize that they've been on the wrong road all along! Suddenly terror sweeps over them. They realize that Jesus Christ really is the Son of God, that the Bible is true, and that they're on their way to everlasting torment.

They've wasted their lives in pursuit of money and pleasures, but suddenly their possessions are gone. Their soul lives for eternity, but no matter how much wealth they accumulated on earth, they have nothing to take with them. As Jesus said, "What profit is it to a man if he gains the whole world, and loses his own soul? Or what will a man give in exchange for his soul?" (Matthew 16:26). They've neglected their spiritual life; which now they realize is more valuable than gold, and they have focused all their time and energy on things that will burn up. What a waste!

They stand trembling before Jesus Christ at the White Throne Judgment. All their wealth on earth does them no good. It's a right standing with God that Jesus demands, and they're sadly lacking. Spiritual matters didn't fit in with their life style on earth and now they're paying the price for their neglect. They wonder how they could have been so foolish. How they wish they could go back to relive their lives, but it's too late. Nothing can be changed.

Suddenly, they look around. Why, there's people here they never expected to see—pastors and others whom they regarded as good church members. Why are they here? These people seemed confused and terrified. Jesus says to them, "Depart from Me for I never knew you."

"But Lord," they cry, "what about the things we did for your kingdom! We preached and taught the Bible. We did much good for the church. Let us in! Let us in!" They frantically scream and wave their hands in the air.

He looks at them sadly and says, "I never knew you. Depart from Me, you workers of iniquity."

Every soul present waits to hear the fate they know is coming. Because they didn't accept Christ's offer of forgiveness for their transgressions, they must pay their own penalty for their sins. The Scripture tells of their eternal doom: "Then Death and Hades were cast into the lake of fire. This is the second death. And anyone not found written in the Book of Life was cast into the lake of fire" (Revelation 20:14–15).

Quick! Let's get off this road. Let's stop and catch our breath after that terrifying journey. No one in their right mind would travel this highway once they realize the final destination.

Let's now travel on the path that leads to everlasting life. But what's this? We can't get on this thoroughfare. The road is blocked. It's our sins that have created a barrier to God. "Your iniquities have separated you from your God" (Isaiah 59:2). We've broken all the Ten Commandments in one way or another; and not only does this prevent us from access to God, but Scripture tells us "the wages of sin is death" (Romans 6:23).

But don't despair—"God demonstrates His own love toward us, in that while we were still sinners, Christ died for us" (Romans 5:8). Jesus can remove the road block of sin if we surrender our lives to Him. All those who put their faith in Him can get on the road that leads to everlasting life.

Let's travel back in time to the crucifixion of Jesus. We can see what it cost Christ to remove that roadblock of sin for us.

As we approach Jerusalem, the sky is filled with dark heavy clouds. Even though it's two o'clock in the afternoon, it appears as if night is falling. It's Passover, and Jews from many countries have crowded into the city for the celebration. As we approach Calvary, we see three men hanging on crosses; the one in the middle is Jesus. His body is bruised and bloody. It's difficult to look at Him; He's clearly in agony, but we're strangely drawn to Him. He gasps for breath as blood streams down His face and sides.

It seems as though everyone in Jerusalem has turned out to witness this event. This is the Man who raised the dead and walked on water. Every eye is now focused on

Him. You hear loud wailing in every direction as men, women, and children cry.

The person next to you says, "That is the Man who opened my blind eyes. What has He done to deserve death?" His sobs blend in with thousands of others.

Suddenly, the earth shakes. Now people's countenances change from grief to terror. Families huddle close together. Someone near you yells, "Is this the end of the world?" Even those who cried, "Crucify Him!" now realize that this is no ordinary Man—and no ordinary death.

Jesus cries out, "My God, My God, why have you forsaken Me?"

God has to turn His back on His beloved Son because Jesus carries the sins of all humanity on Himself.

Just before Jesus dies, the veil of the temple is torn from top to bottom, allowing access to God through the death of Christ. At the very hour that the priest slaughters the Passover lamb, the Lamb of God says, "It is finished." God's plan of redemption is complete. The sinless Son of God voluntarily died for the sins of the world. In three days, He will be resurrected for His Bride, the Church.

> "Surely He has borne our griefs and carried our sorrows; yet we esteemed Him stricken, smitten by God, and afflicted. But He was wounded for our transgressions, He was bruised for our iniquities; the chastisement for our peace was upon Him, and by His stripes we are healed. All we like sheep have gone astray; we have turned, every one to his own way; and the Lord has laid on Him the iniquity of us all."
> Isaiah 53:4–6

Jesus suffered a horrible death for us. It was His love for us that led Him to the cross. It was His death that removed the road block of sin that keeps us from entering the path to everlasting life.

Are there any restrictions to getting on this highway?

All who put their faith in Christ are welcome on the road to eternal life. It doesn't matter how badly you've messed up, Christ will forgive you and even forget what you've done. He's not concerned about your race or nationality either. You could have been a Muslim, a Buddhist, or have no religion at all. All are welcome in God's family, for He is "not willing that any should perish but that all should come to repentance" (2 Peter 3:9). God has done all He can do to get people off the road that leads to destruction and on to the path of everlasting life. He went so far as to give His only Son to die in our place. What more could He have done?

I believe in Jesus. Doesn't that mean I'm a Christian?

The only entrance into God's kingdom is to repent and place your faith in Christ. "For by grace you have been saved through faith, and that not of yourselves; it is the gift of God, not of works, lest anyone should boast" (Ephesians 2:8–9). Even if you've been baptized and are a member of a church, you're still not a Christian until you've been born again. Jesus told Nicodemus, "Most assuredly, I say to you, unless one is born again, he cannot see the kingdom of God" (John 3:3). If you've never done that, there's no better time than right now.

You might have grown up in the church. You might have gone through catechism, and accepted all that your parents and the church believe. But that's not enough. You must examine your faith. Is it real? Think through everything you've been taught. Do you really believe Jesus is the Son of God.? Is the Bible really true? Don't become a Christian because your parents expect you to. Do it because you believe Jesus is who He claimed to be, and you want Him to be the Lord of your life. Your faith will not be truly your own until you examine it and make sure you believe it. You can't get on the highway to everlasting life by your parents' or your grandparents' faith.

You get on the road to eternal life by placing you faith in Christ. If you haven't and you want to, you can pray right now to receive Christ. Don't worry if you don't know how to pray. You don't need to use fancy words. Just talk to God the same way you talk to a friend. The following prayer can help you or you could use your own words.

"Dear Jesus, I have sinned against you. I'm sorry for my past sins. Please forgive me. I know you died for me. Come into my heart. I give my life to you. Thank you for saving me."

Once you have given your heart to the Lord, you've made the most important decision of your life. It's more important than getting married or choosing a career. Marriage and a career are life-long decisions, but salvation lasts forever.

But how can I be sure I'm saved? Sometimes, I don't feel like I'm a Christian.

Don't rely on your feelings. Rely on the truth that's in

God's Word. You can be sure you're a Christian if you sincerely prayed to ask Christ into your heart. The Scripture tells us,

> "This is the testimony: that God has given us eternal life, and this life is in His Son. He who has the Son has life; he who does not have the Son of God does not have life. These things I have written to you who believe in the name of the Son of God, that you may know that you have eternal life, and that you may continue to believe in the name of the Son of God."
>
> 1 John 5:11–13

Those who are truly a child of God want to study the Bible. "As newborn babes, desire the pure milk of the word, that you may grow thereby, if indeed you have tasted that the Lord is gracious" (1 Peter 2:2–3). You know you're a Christian if you have a desire to study the Bible.

You also have the Holy Spirit living within you. He will convict you of sin and help you live a holy life. With the Spirit of God with you, you won't feel comfortable breaking God's commandments as you did before. When the Holy Spirit convicts you of sin, you'll know for sure that you're a child of God.

After I accept Christ, does that mean I'll have no problems or sin in my life?

No matter which road of life you choose to travel, you'll have trials and temptations. Every human being struggles with these as long as they live. But we have an important advantage over nonbelievers—Christ helps us through each difficulty. "Call upon Me in the day of trouble; I will deliver you, and you shall glorify Me" (Psalm 50:15).

After we accept Christ, we still battle sin and temptation even though we're a new creation in Christ. That's because we still have the old sin nature in us. When we do sin, we need to ask God to forgive us. "If we confess our sins, He is faithful and just to forgive our sins and to cleanse us from all unrighteousness" (1 John 1:9). Once we confess our sin and forsake it, God completely forgives and even forgets what we've done. There's much more about overcoming temptation in the chapter on spiritual warfare.

Troubles and temptations have a purpose—they test us. Paul says, "We also glory in tribulations, knowing that tribulation produces perseverance; and perseverance, character, and character, hope" (Romans 5:3–4). These cause real pain, and being a Christian doesn't give us immunity from sufferings. These problems strengthen our faith in God, and draw us closer to Him. We learn things during times of pain and suffering that we would never learn any other way.

Some Christians abandon their faith when difficulties come. They don't see God's ultimate plan in affliction. Instead of seeing suffering as a way to draw closer to God, they become discouraged; stop attending church, and eventually abandon their faith all together. The problem that was intended to draw them closer to Christ drives them away. They don't understand that the church, the Bible and prayer can help them through each crisis they encounter.

We can have victory over difficulties when Christ is the center of our lives. When we turn difficulties over to the Lord, He takes control. He brings about the best possible solution to every situation. He's a prayer-answering, miracle-working God. When our struggle is over, we rejoice in what our heavenly Father has done. This brings glory to God, and causes others to be encouraged. Christians can live triumphantly even in difficult situations when Christ is in control of their lives.

The book of Acts records the story of a man who had been lame from birth. As he was begging at the temple one day, Peter and John walked by. The beggar looked up expecting to receive alms. Peter said to him, "Silver and gold I do not have, but what I do have I give you: In the name of Jesus Christ of Nazareth, rise up and walk" (Acts 3:6).

Peter helped the man stand up, and then he took some steps. The lame man was so excited over being healed that he walked, leaped, and praised God! Everyone around him praised God, too.

That's what happens when we give a situation over to the Lord, and He takes control. Our problem gets solved, people praise God, and He gets the glory.

During our Wednesday night service at Evangel Temple, the pastor gives the congregation an opportunity to tell what God has done for them during the week. People relate how God answered their prayers. Some have had marriages restored or a prodigal son or daughter return to the Lord. Others have been spared surgery because God healed them. Not every person has all of their difficulties solved, but many do. When this happens, the entire congregation rejoices. This encourages others who are facing difficulties—they know that God is still in the miracle-working business.

Now don't think God brings difficulties on us so that He can receive glory. God does allow problems to test us and to draw us closer to Him. As long as we're in this world, we will have problems; but thankfully, we have Christ with us to help us through each one. "The name of the Lord is a strong tower; the righteous run to it and are safe" (Proverbs 18:10). We can live triumphantly in spite of difficulties if we put our trust in Him.

The Natural Man, the Carnal Man, and the Spiritual Man

Some Christians want to get on the path to everlasting life, but still hold on to their old sin nature. They want to live for the flesh the way a natural man does who doesn't know Christ. Paul refers to this type of believer as a carnal Christian. He's still a babe in Christ no matter how long he's been a believer. He does the same things that the natural man does (Man refers to either man or woman). He wants to live for the world and also live for Christ. The world calls him a hypocrite. The carnal Christian can't please God, nor can he have real intimacy with Him. Paul tells us,

> "For those who live according to the flesh set their minds on the things of the flesh, but those who live according to the Spirit, the things of the Spirit. For to be carnally minded is death, but to be spiritually minded is life and peace. Because the carnal mind is enmity against God; for it is not subject to the law of God, nor indeed can be. So then, those who are in the flesh cannot please God."
>
> Romans 8:5–8

You can easily spot the carnal man; he's the one who doesn't have joy and peace in his life; he's a pitiful person. The carnal Christian can never live triumphantly. He's too bogged down with sin. Paul tells us, "He who sows to his flesh will of the flesh reap corruption, but he who sows to the Spirit will of the Spirit reap everlasting life" (Galatians 6:8).

Is the carnal man really saved? John tells us, "He who says, 'I know Him,' and does not keep His commandments, is a liar, and the truth is not in him. But whoever keeps His word, truly the love of God is perfect in him. By this we know that we are in Him" (1 John 2:4–5). In the end, Paul tells us that "to be carnally minded is death" (Romans 8:6).

Let's look at the spiritual man. He's tempted just as the natural and carnal man; but because he walks in the Spirit, he's able to have victory over temptation. Walking in the Spirit means to be controlled by the Holy Spirit rather than the flesh. The spiritual man spends adequate time daily in prayer and Bible study. He has God's Word hidden in his heart and the Holy Spirit helps him when he's tempted. You can easily spot the spiritual man. He's the one with love, joy, peace, long-suffering, patience, goodness, kindness, faithfulness, and self-control. Because he's obedient, God can use him in His kingdom. That's the only kind of person God can use to accomplish His work. God is looking for Christians that are obedient to Him. Those are the individuals that live triumphantly.

We're all in a life-long process of becoming holy. Our ultimate goal is to be formed in the likeness of God's Son. The process we go through to achieve holiness is called sanctification. I never fully understood sanctification until I heard Dr. D. James Kennedy use an illustration that helped me grasp its meaning in a way that I will never forget. He told about an unruly youth who came before a judge. This boy had a foul mouth and a long history of breaking the law. The judge eventually adopted him as his own son. Now that judge had his work cut out for him! That unruly teenager had a lot of changes to make in his life. It took much persuasion and discipline to turn that boy into a productive citizen.

That's the way sanctification works for us. When we come to Christ, we're like that unruly teenager. We want to follow our own fleshly desires, but God wants us to be holy. In fact, without holiness, we can't please God; but our own sinful nature prevents us from achieving it. Sanctification is the process God uses to make us acceptable to Him. He has to train and discipline us to make us holy. We all go through a life-long process of changing from our old sinful nature into holiness. And God uses the Bible to accomplish this. Paul tells us,

> "That He might sanctify and cleanse her with the washing of water by the word, that He might present her to Himself a glorious church, not having spot or wrinkle or any such thing, but that she should be holy and without blemish."
>
> Ephesians 5:26–27

God is changing us into the likeness of His Son, and He uses the washing of the Word to do it. That's one of the core purposes of the Bible—to teach us holiness. You know how clean and refreshed you feel when you step out of the shower each morning. That's what the Bible does for our soul. When we study the Scripture and apply its teachings to our lives, the old sin nature is washed away. Our soul feels clean and refreshed just as though we have given our soul a bath. That's what it means to be washed in the Word, and we need it every day. God wants you to be holy, and He's given you everything you need to know about achieving it in the Bible.

As I think back over my life, I'm reminded of how patient God had been to me in the process of sanctification. Many times I've failed Him, but He hasn't given up on me. Through discipline and pruning, He's helped me grow from one spiritual level to the next.

Understanding the process of sanctification has helped me be more patient with other Christians. We're all under construction and we're at different levels of growth. We're always pressing higher and higher to be formed into the image of God's Son.

If only you knew how much God loves you! It's impossible for us to comprehend God's great love. We can't fathom it. We try to comprehend God's love with our limited minds, but we can't do it. We're so limited. God is limitless. No wonder we humans don't love God as we should. God understands our limitations. He remembers that we're dust. He also knows what's in our hearts. He knows a heart that is turned towards Him. David was that kind of person. He was a man after God's own heart. That's the kind of person God is looking for.

God loves you so much that He desires to lavish His great love and goodness on you. You're so special to Him that it's His desire to bless every area of your life. He wants to do more for you than you can even think or imagine. There's one condition to these blessings—you must love God and put Him first in your life. When you put Him first in all things, He is able to pour out His blessings on your family, your finances, your job, and everything else. You can have a joyful and abundant life if you love God and put Him first.

What can God do with a person who loves Him, and puts Him first in their life? We can find out by looking in the Bible. Moses disobeyed God. David was a murderer and an adulterer. Peter denied Jesus. Every person in the Scripture except Jesus was flawed in some way. They were ordinary people just like you and me. They at times were disobedient just as we've been, but God was able to use them in spite of their imperfections. God's work on earth gets done by imperfect people who love God and surrender their lives to Him.

God loves us in spite of our imperfections. When we think of God's love and goodness to us, it should cause us to love Him wholeheartedly. But I know from my own experience, loving God isn't always easy. I think this is difficult for most of us because we can't see God. I knew Jesus said, "You shall love the Lord your God with all your heart, with all your soul, and with all your mind" (Matthew 22:37), but I didn't.

Then, my former pastor's wife, Mabel Walker, told me of someone she knew who wanted to love God, but she didn't. This woman put into practice the Bible verse, "God who...calls those things which do not exist as though they did" (Romans 4:17). Each day she said, "I love you, Lord." After about three weeks, she actually did.

I did as she had done. Each day, I said, "I love you, Lord." Soon I really did love God.

I was finally giving God what He wanted most from me—that I love Him above all else.

Is there anything you love more than God? It could be your family, money, your pets, or even football. If there's anything you love more than God, it's an idol; and He can remove it. "You shall have no other gods before Me" (Exodus 20:3). God wants first place in every area of your life.

Until Jesus has complete control, you will never be all you can be. That means you must let Christ have dominion over even those secret areas that no one knows about. He is either Lord of all or not Lord at all. If you can't seem to conquer a particular sin or addiction in your life, perhaps you need additional help. There's a chapter on spiritual warfare later in this book that can help you. Once we surrender all to Him, we position ourselves for total victory.

Thy Word is a Lamp unto Mine Feet

Come travel back in time to one of the most exciting events in Jewish history. The Children of Israel were about to enter the Promised Land. Forty years of wondering in the desert were over. They were ready to enter Canaan, and Joshua would lead them. Just before they crossed the Jordan River, God gave Joshua these instructions:

> "Only be strong and very courageous, that you may observe to do according to all the law which Moses My servant commanded you; do not turn from it to the right hand or to the left, that you may prosper wherever you go. This Book of the Law shall not depart from your mouth, but you shall meditate in it day and night, that you may observe to do according to all that is written in it. For then you will make your way prosperous, and then you will have good success."
>
> Joshua 1:7–8

Wow! Joshua was guaranteed victory in conquering Canaan. Not only would he have success, but *good* success. And he would prosper—*but only if he kept all of God's laws and meditated on them continually.*

That promised wasn't just for Joshua—it's for you, too; for whatever was written in the Bible is for our benefit. Yes, you can be guaranteed to prosper and have good success, but only if you keep God's commandments and meditate on His Laws day and night.

Wait a minute! I couldn't do that. Keeping all God's commandments and meditating on them all the time is too difficult. I'm sure not Joshua.

God wouldn't ask you to do something if it was impossible to accomplish. You can do it. God will be with you and work through you to achieve His purpose. And He will help you live a holy life dedicated to Him. Sure, you'll face trials and temptations, but God will be with you to help you. And you will no doubt stumble once in a while; we all do. When you do, get back on track quickly. We'll never be sinless in this life as Jesus was, but that should be our goal. Each day, we should strive to be like Him in all we do. And we learn how to be like Jesus from studying the Bible.

So what makes the Bible so special? Can't I have success by reading other books?

You could go to the library or book store to find books on achieving success, but they'll only take you so far. If you want success God's way, you must follow His instructions; and they're only found in the Scripture. The verse in the exact center of the Bible is quite important and it speaks to this matter. "It is better to trust in the Lord than to put confidence in man" (Psalm 118: 8).

There never has been nor ever will be another book like the Bible. The Bible is a unique collection of sixty-six books, written by about thirty-nine men. The Holy Spirit guided them as they wrote. "All Scripture is given by inspiration of God, and is profitable for doctrine, for reproof, for correction, for instruction in righteousness, that the man of God may be complete, thoroughly equipped for every good work" (2 Timothy 3:16–17).

The word inspiration means the Bible was "God breathed." Even though the books of the Bible were written over many centuries by different men, their messages all agree. That's because the Holy Spirit guided them as they wrote.

Within the pages of the Bible is everything you need to know to live a victorious Christian life. The Scripture will correct you when you're in error, and give you guidance in every situation you face.

Why did God give us the Bible?

God has revealed Himself through the Scriptures. We can know who He is and something of His nature by reading the Word. Through it, God reveals His plan from creation to the ages to come. The Bible also tells us God's plan to redeem mankind. From the Scriptures, we know that Jesus died for our sin. The Bible also gives us rules to live by. It is an instruction book for life.

Isn't the Bible just one of several books that show us truth?

All major world religions have sacred writings, but the Bible is the only one that has the answers to mankind's deepest need—how to have a relationship with his Creator. No other sacred book has God's plan to send His Son to die for our sins. It is from the Scripture that we find, "For God so loved the world that He gave His only begotten Son, that whoever believes in Him should not perish but have everlasting life" (John 3:16). The Bible is the only book that is inspired by God, and tells us where we came from and where we're going.

Is the entire Bible true?

Yes it is! The entire Word of God is from God and contains no error. Some people don't believe this. For example, they teach that the creation of the world as described in the first chapter of Genesis is a myth. If we say that some of the Bible is true and other portions aren't, where do we draw the line? Who's to say what is true and what isn't? All Scripture is inspired as we read in 2 Timothy 3:16, "All Scripture is given by inspiration of God, and is profitable for reproof, for correction, for instruction in righteousness."

Not only is the Bible inspired by God, but it's also living and active. This is an important point, and it makes the Bible unique. No other book is alive and active. The words in the Bible have the power of God in them. As you read the Scriptures, its words will penetrate your heart as no other words can. "For the Word of God is living and powerful, and sharper than any two-edged sword, piercing even to the division of soul and spirit, and of joints and marrow, and is a discerner of the thoughts and intents of the heart" (Hebrews 4:12).

Two people could read the same passages, but they might be affected in different ways because the words would get down into their "joints and marrow" that is, their soul and spirit, and speak to them according to what's going on in their lives. It will discern their thoughts, convict them of sin (if needed) and correct them if they were in error. No other written words have that power. That's because the Bible has the power of God in it. It's the same power that's in the name of Jesus and the blood of Jesus.

The Bible is unique in another way—it alone contains the power to defeat the devil. God's Word is our only offensive weapon to attack the unholy trinity—Satan, the flesh, and the world. All evil forces are forced to flee when God's Word is used against them.

As you do something for God, you can be sure the devil will try to stop you. That's what happened to Jesus when He began his public ministry. He used Scripture to defeat the devil and you can too. (See Matthew 4:1–11.) If the devil tempted the Son of God, you can be sure he'll attack you, too. Don't worry. You have the Sword of the Lord, the Bible, to defeat his attacks. You'll find more about this in the chapter on spiritual warfare.

Aren't you glad God gave us the Bible? As we've seen, it's unique in many ways. The book of Proverbs tells us what we can expect when we read and obey God's Word. "My son, do not forget my law, but let your heart keep my commands; for length of days and long life and peace they will add to you" Proverbs 3:1–2. Everything you need to know about life is written within its pages for it will equip you for every good work.

I listen to a sermon on Sunday mornings. Is that's all the Bible study I need?

That's all the Bible study many Christians receive; but that's not enough to keep you strong in the Lord. If you want the Bible to change your life, you need to study it every day. You can't be physically strong by eating once a week; you can't be spiritually strong by feeding your soul only on Sunday morning sermons. If you want to be strong in the Lord, you must read the Bible daily.

Reading the Bible is beneficial, but it's even better to study it. For this, you'll need a good study Bible. In it, you'll find information that explains Scripture passages verse by verse. You can also purchase Bible study material written by competent Bible teachers. These can be bought at any Christian book store. Also, most churches have Bible study groups and adult Sunday school classes to help you. These groups shouldn't replace daily Bible study, though. Whether you study the Bible alone, with your partner or with the entire family, it's well worth the time you put into it.

But I don't have time for Bible study.

Bible study doesn't need to take long. In fact, it's better to read a few verses; meditate on them, and apply them to your life rather than read a large portion and not think about what you're reading. If you can find time to eat each day, you can find a few minutes to feed your soul on God's Word.

You'll be amazed at the changes spending time with the Lord in Bible study and prayer will bring to you. You'll have God's wisdom within you. This will cause some major changes in your life. You'll face every challenge with confidence, knowing God will guide you through every difficult situation. Your face will shine and your eyes will sparkle. People who met you will know that you've been with the Lord and see that His Word lives in you. Aren't these all great reasons to get into God's Word every day? In fact, your Bible study time might turn out to be the best part of your day!

I have always read the Bible daily, but sometimes I did it merely out of obligation. I would hurriedly read a chapter, but not wholeheartedly. Then something happened that made me take the Bible seriously. I saw what is happening in the world today foretold centuries ago in the Bible. The Scriptures state that Israel would once again become a nation; and that in the end days, mankind would become violent and wicked. As I saw these events take place, I knew that I needed to take the Bible seriously. I began a diligent study of the Scriptures. I asked God to show me every truth that is in His Word. God must have been pleased with that request because as I studied and applied the things I learned, my life was transformed. I developed a deeper walk with God, and received power from the Holy Spirit. My marriage has improved; I'm happier and healthier, too. Perhaps the greatest change is that God is working through me to achieve His purpose for my life. All of this came about by one request—to know what was in the Bible. I set out to discover facts, but I received so much more. Except for the prayer to ask Christ into my heart, that was the most important prayer I ever prayed. I know that what the Bible has done for me, it can do for anyone.

Pardon me for a moment. I want to pause right now and thank God for His Word. I'm overwhelmed when I think of how the Bible has impacted not only my life, but millions of others as well.

> "Dear God, thank you for Your precious Holy Word. I know You because You have revealed Yourself to me in the Bible. Thank you for giving me Your plan from creation to the ages to come. You have also revealed in it Your deep love for me. You have given me rules to live by—rules not to restrict me, but to give me happiness within the boundaries you have set. My life is filled with joy because of Your Word. The Bible tells me that some day, I will stand before Your judgment seat with my sins forgiven because Jesus paid for my salvation at the cross. My home in heaven and my rewards are described within its pages. Thank you for telling me where I came from and where I'm going.
>
> "I pray that every person who reads this will be transformed by the power that is in Your Word. May You bless each one and bring them into a deep commitment to You."

Isn't the Bible outdated?

The Bible is God's Word for all time. It's the final authority on all matters. It's never out of date, and it never changes. This is important for Christians to grasp in today's world. Our standard can't be what the world is doing; our standard must be the Word of God.

How can I get my children interested in studying the Bible?

When you're enthusiastic about the Scripture, they'll be, too. Talk about Bible verses often. Let them see you read God's Word and apply biblical truth to situations throughout the day. Then have a time to study the Scripture together as a family. Children love hearing exciting stories, singing songs or hymns, and review what they've learned in a game. They'll have so much fun that they won't realize the important truths they're learning.

Proverbs 22:6 tells us that if we train up our children in the way they should go, when they are old, they will not depart from it. Do you want your children to live by God's standards or the world's? The only way they will learn to live by God's rules is if you teach them, and they see you consistently applying biblical truths to your own life. That's the reason the Bible tells us, "You shall lay up these words of mine in your heart and in your soul…You shall teach them to your children, speaking of them when you sit in your house, when you walk by the way, when you lie down, and when you rise up" (Deuteronomy 11:18–19).

Why are there so many translations of the Bible? And which one is the best?

There are many translations of the Bible, and it can be confusing when it comes time to choosing one. Many people prefer the Authorized King James Version of the

Bible. I once worked in a Christian bookstore, and I sold many Bibles. One elderly lady came in and said, "I want a King James Bible. I don't want one of those new translations. I want the one the Lord spoke!" That dear lady didn't know Jesus spoke Aramaic, and that most of the New Testament was written in Greek. (The Old Testament was written in Hebrew.)

The King James Bible has been a favorite of Christians for generations. But we don't speak Elizabethan English now; and it's difficult to understand. That's the reason we have modern translations. *The New International Version,* the *Revised Standard Version,* and the *New King James* are just some of them. Many people like the *Living Bible,* which is a paraphrase, that is, the meaning has been put into our modern language. I personally like the *New King James* because it's close to the Authorized King James Version, easy to memorize, and easy to understand. Whatever translation you get is fine as long as you like it. If you like it, then you'll want to study it.

What's the difference between the Old Testament and the New Testament? And is the Old Testament still relevant today?

The Old Testament is a history of God's chosen people, the Jews. God chose Jewish prophets to write the Holy Scriptures. And it's from the Jewish race that God sent the Redeemer of mankind. The promised Savior is written about extensively in the books of Psalm and Isaiah. And He's mentioned in many other Old Testament books. We can't fully understand the life of Christ until we understand the Old Testament. Someone once wrote that the

New Testament is in the Old Testament concealed, and the Old Testament is in the New Testament revealed.

The first four books of the New Testament tells about the life of Jesus—His birth, ministry and death. These are called the Gospels—Matthew, Mark, Luke, and John. The rest of the New Testament tells about the church. The Book of Acts gives the history of the church; the remaining are letters written to the churches. The last book, Revelation, tells what will happen at the end of this age and Christ's return.

Is it your desire to have a deeper commitment to God? The only way this can happen is through Bible study. There's no short-cut to intimacy with God. You must spend time with Him in prayer and Bible study. God will speak to you and direct your path as long as you stay in His Word. The Bible will guide your path, but only if you study it and apply its teaching to your life. "Your word is a lamp to my feet and a light to my path" (Psalm 119:105).

Not only should you study the Scripture daily, you're instructed to meditate on it day and night. Here's what you can expect to happen when you do:

> "Blessed is the man who walks not in the council of the ungodly, nor stands in the path of sinners, nor sits in the seat of the scornful; but his delight is in the law of the Lord, and in His law he meditates day and night. He shall be like a tree planted by the rivers of water, that brings forth its fruit in its season, whose leaf also shall not wither; and whatever he does shall prosper."
>
> Psalm 1:1–3

If you want to live triumphantly, these verses tell you how to do it—meditate on God's Word. Fill your mind with verses from the Bible throughout the day. Whatever you're doing, think of a verse that applies. Whenever an attitude or thought comes to your mind that isn't pleasing to God, cast it down and replace it.

> "Whatever things are true, whatever things are noble, whatever things are just, whatever things are pure, whatever things are lovely, whatever things are of good report, if there is any virtue and if there is anything praiseworthy—meditate on these things."
>
> Philippians 4:8

This is the only way to keep your mind clear and focused on God. Then you will truly live an abundant life.

Not only are you to study and meditate on the Bible, but you should memorize it. "Your word I have hidden in my heart, that I might not sin against You" (Psalm 119:11). God's Word will keep you from sin, but only if you have hidden it in your heart.

There's one more thing you need to do—obey it. "Be doers of the Word and not hearers only" (James 1:22). It will do you no good to study the Bible if you don't apply it to your life. I've learned from experience that's the only way to God's blessings.

After reading this chapter, don't you appreciate the Bible more than you did before? I know I do. I'm thankful that God gave us the Scripture. If you're a Christian and have a copy of the Bible along with the ability to read it, and the privilege to worship God openly; you are blessed indeed! Millions of people around the world don't.

Twelve Keys to Effective Praying

When Catherine Marshal was preparing for college, she had everything she needed—everything, that is, except money for tuition. It was during the Great Depression, and her father was a Presbyterian minister. Times were difficult; their family was barely scraping by. Her father usually had to buy groceries on credit by the end of the week. How could she ever get money for schooling? It was at that time that her mother taught her about her "secret account" where all their emergency funding came from. They knelt beside Catherine's bed and prayed. This wasn't the usual short prayer that Catherine heard before meals. This prayer was long and intense, crying out to the Lord.

A few days later, her mother received a letter from an editor who asked her to write about her experiences as a teacher in Appalachia. The money she received was more than enough to pay Catherine's tuition. (Many years later, this material was put into a book by Catherine Marshal called *Christy*.) [1]

Catherine Marshall's mother knew how to approach the throne of God to meet her every need.

God doesn't answer my prayers like that. I suppose only a few people ever get their prayers answered as she did.

You can get your prayers answered just as Catherine Marshall's mother did for "God shows no partiality" (Acts 10:34). That means He'll answer the prayers of anyone who asks according to the instructions given in His Word. In this chapter, we'll discover twelve keys that will unlock the power of prayer for you. We'll also see that prayer is more than asking; it's the way into the very heart of God.

Frederick K.C. Price said, "Prayer is a means of communication and contact with your heavenly Father. Combined with faith in God's Word, prayer is a channel through which and by which His power can be released to meet our needs, allowing Him to get involved in our circumstances." [2]

Did you catch that? God's power is released though prayer. Prayer is the only way God can help us. John Wesley made this statement: "It seems God is limited by our prayer life—that He can do nothing for humanity unless someone asks Him."

If God is all-powerful, why can't He act until someone prays?

It's true that God is sovereign over the universe. He places governments and leaders in power, but He limits Himself as to what He can do. That's because God gave Adam dominion over the earth. When Adam sinned, Satan gained control of this world system. (God still is sovereign over the universe.) You can read about this in the third chapter of Genesis. Satan is referred to as the god of this world (see 2 Corinthians 4:4). The world is now under Satan's dominion. In order for God to make changes in the world, people must pray. He has the power to do more than we can ask or even image, but God can't act until someone prays.

That means your prayers are important! When you go to your room, close the door and pray, you are moving the hand of God. You can move mountains and change lives. You can bring blessings to your children, healing to the sick, and wisdom to the President, congress and other national leaders. You can ask God to help troubled marriages, bring prosperity to your work or business, and aide persecuted Christians around the world. You can bring power and wisdom to your pastor. You can pray that your neighborhood would be free of drugs and crime. Your prayers, combined with those of other Christians, can tear down strongholds of demonic forces in this nation; and help America return to God. Whatever concerns you have can be brought before your heavenly Father. Since prayer is such serious business, it deserves your best effort. Is there anything you do that is more important than prayer?

Every person finds what they need when they come to the Father. The troubled soul finds peace; the repentant sinner receives forgiveness; the lonely experience comfort; the prodigal is completely restored. All who thirst for a deeper relationship with God find it when they come to Him in prayer.

To get the most out of it, prayer requires preparation. In her book, *Experiencing God through Prayer,* Madame Guyon explains the preparation for prayer.

"When you have settled into a peaceful spirit and are fully aware of God's presence; when earthly distractions are not your primary thoughts; when your soul has properly fed on God's Word and you have chosen by an act of your will to believe it, you are now ready to communicate with your heavenly Father."[3]

As Madame Guyon suggests, prayer requires preparation. Do you have a quiet place where you can get alone with your heavenly Father to pray? This is one of the most important times of your day. After all, it's your appointment with the King of the Universe, and it requires your best effort.

After you've settled into your favorite place, you're ready to talk to your heavenly Father. Let's now look at twelve keys that will make that time more affective.

The first key: Pray in secret

Jesus said, "When you pray, go into your room, and when you have shut your door, pray to your Father who is in the secret place; and your Father who sees in secret will reward you openly" (Matthew 6:6).

The Pharisees of Jesus' day loved to stand on street corners and say long prayers in public. People walked by and admired their piety. Jesus said that they have received their reward. All who pray to impress others receive the praises of men. When we pray in secret, God rewards us openly.

When you pray in secret, you don't have to be concerned about impressing others or about what someone else thinks. When you get alone with God, it's only the two of you. There's no need to impress Him with fancy words or use "thees" or "thous." Just talk to God respectfully, keeping in mind that He is holy and the sovereign ruler of the universe. You should approach God with awe and reverence at all times; never take Him casually.

Even though He is awesome and holy, He loves you and longs for you to spend time with Him. You can pour out your heart and be totally honest with God; after all, He knows all about you. He knows things that no one else knows. You can confess your sins, your weaknesses, and fears. You can tell Him things that you wouldn't tell anyone else.

When Jesus said we should pray in secret, did He mean we shouldn't pray in public?

Jesus meant we shouldn't pray to impress others. Public prayers are powerful when they're prayed sincerely. The purpose of public prayers should be to glorify God and move His hand into action. Jesus said, "My house shall be called a house of prayer" (Matthew 21:13). Corporate prayers are quite effective because the greater the number of people praying in agreement, the greater is the release of God's power. God is longing to pour out blessings on churches who meet together to pray. It's these congregations who receive manifestations of the Holy Spirit; and through His power, mighty works can be done. Yes, corporate prayers are affective when people humble themselves and seek God's face, and not merely pray to impress others. There's more on this subject of corporate prayers in the chapter titled, "The Glorious Church, the Bride of Christ."

The second key: Seek God early in the morning

> "My voice You shall hear in the morning, O Lord; in the morning I will direct it to You, and I will look up."
>
> Psalm 5:3

Many people say a short prayer at the end of the day; some pray only when they're in trouble. That kind of praying is ineffective. I used to say a short prayer before I fell asleep, but it seemed that God seldom heard me. I've discovered that if I want to move the hand of God, I have to make praying a priority. Now I pray early in the morning, and I've found the dynamic power that's in prayer.

There are advantages to starting your day with prayer. First, your time with the Lord doesn't get crowded out because of a busy schedule. Also, by staring your day with the Lord, you'll have His presence and help all day long.

But it's impossible for me to pray early in the morning. Can't I pray at any other time of day?

It's far more important that you pray rather than when you pray. I believe that starting your day with a quiet time with the Lord is best, but if that's not practical, then pray whenever it fits your schedule. Some people pray while their children are napping, or when they're on their lunch hour, or in the evening. Find the time that's best for you. Even five minutes of fervent praying is better than not praying at all.

When you're going through a crisis, you'll find that praying once a day isn't enough. The Psalmist tells us "Evening and morning and at noon will I pray, and cry aloud, and He shall hear my voice. He has redeemed my soul in peace from the battle that was against me" (Psalm 55:17–18). Are you facing a battle right now? Crying out to God three times a day will help you and give you peace instead of turmoil.

The third key: Effective praying requires a consecrated life. "He who called you is holy, you also be holy in all your conduct, because it is written, 'Be holy, for I am holy'" (1 Peter 1:15–16).

I enjoy reading biographies of famous Christians. When I study the lives of people who have accomplished much for God, I'm inspired to do my best. I've noticed that they all have some common characteristic. Every person that achieves great things for God lives a consecrated life and spends much time in prayer. No one ever truly triumphs in the Christian life without these two.

What does it mean to live a consecrated life? In his book, *The Complete Works of E. M. Bounds,* he says, "Consecration is the voluntary set dedication of one's self to God, an offering definitely made, and made without any reservation whatever. It is the setting apart of all we are, all we have, and all we expect to have or be, to God first of all." [4]

Those who have such a commitment to God get their prayers answered. I like the way E. M. Bounds describes this person.

> "Consecration is really the setting apart of one's self to a life of prayer. It means not only to pray, but to pray habitually, and to pray more effectually. It is the consecrated man who accomplishes most by his

praying. God must hear the man wholly given up to God. God cannot deny the request of him who has renounced all claims to himself, and who has wholly dedicated himself to God and his service."⁵

God desires that you live triumphantly. He wants to bless you abundantly. And this will only happen if your life is totally consecrated to God. God can't use Christians who have a half-hearted commitment. Every person who has ever accomplished something great for God's kingdom has had a consecrated life. And a consecrated life is one given to much prayer.

But I can only talk to God about two or three minutes, and then I can't think of anything else to say.

Many people don't know how to pray beyond two or three minutes. When you finish reading this chapter, you'll find enough to fill up an entire hour or more!

The fourth key: Worship God.

> "But the hour is coming and now is, when the true worshipers will worship the Father in spirit and truth; for the Father is seeking such to worship Him. God is Spirit, and those who worship Him must worship in spirit and truth."
>
> John 4:23–24

Would you like to have the joy of the Lord with you the entire day? Would you like the presence and power of the Holy Spirit with you also? Well, you can. You can have the joy of the Lord and the Spirit's power when you start you prayer time worshipping God.

The majority of Christians miss out on the daily presence of the Holy Spirit because they believe worship is only for Sunday mornings. Worship should be part of every quiet time with the Lord. Tell God that you love Him. Thank Him for what He has done. Sing a song of praise or a hymn.

Psalm 33:3 tells us to sing a new song to the Lord. I discovered what it means to sing a new song when I read Ruth Heflin's book *Glory*. In her book, she explains that singing a new song refers to creating a song as you worship God. That means making up your own words and melody. I was skeptical of this at first since I have no musical ability. But I soon discovered that even I can make up a few lines of praise. This doesn't have to be elaborate. A short chorus works well. She explained that when we sing a familiar song, our mind wonders. When we sing a chorus we have just composed, we keep our minds focused on worshipping. I've found that it really does help me to keep focused on worship.

God is worthy of our wholehearted worship. When we truly worship, God rewards us with His presence, His peace, and His power. God wants to lavish His goodness and love upon us, but it's only when we truly worship Him that He is able to do so. He'll perform miracles and give us the desires of our hearts. "I will praise You, O Lord, with my whole heart; I will tell of all Your marvelous works. I will be glad and rejoice in You; I will sing praise to Your name, O Most High" (Psalm 9:1–2).

The fifth key: Simply ask for what you need

"You do not have because you do not ask."

James 4:2

How often God wants to give us all we need and much of what we desire, but we never ask. In his book, *The Prayer of Jabez,* Bruce Wilkinson tells a fable of Mr. Jones, who went to heaven and saw a large building resembling a warehouse. He discovered that the building contained white boxes tied with red ribbon. Each box had a name on it. Mr. Jones found one that belonged to him. Inside were all the things God wanted to give him while he was on earth, but he never asked. How heartbroken Mr. Jones was when he realized all he could have had during his life time.[6]

Not only is God a loving heavenly Father, but He is also generous to His children. He doesn't want us to lack any good thing. His plan is that we ask and He supplies. In the Lord's Prayer, Jesus told His disciples to ask for their daily bread. God could give us everything we need without our asking, but His plan is that we ask. I believe He did this so that we would know we are dependant on Him for our every need. "Ask, and you will receive, that your joy may be full" (John 16:24).

As I pray, I close my eyes and imagine that I'm talking to God as He sits on His throne. This mental image keeps me focused on what I'm saying and prevents my mind from wondering.

The sixth key: Ask in Jesus' name

> Jesus said, "If you ask anything in My name, I will do it."
>
> John 14:14

There's power and authority in Jesus' name, and it's available to us when we pray. Praying in the name of Jesus gives us the power of attorney to take care of matters in the kingdom of God. Have you ever had power of attorney for someone? If you have, you know you can write checks and handle the finances for another person, just as he or she does. If I had the power of attorney for my brother, I could write checks from his account to pay his bills. I could also take care of legal matters for him. As his power of attorney, I would be authorized to take care of all his business. As a child of God, you have the power of attorney to take care of kingdom business for Jesus Christ. Jesus is no longer present in bodily form to do the things He once did. We are now his representatives on earth to do His work.

We can ask God to do the things that Jesus would do if He were here. Since we are asking for official business of the King, our prayers should line up with the will of God. "Whatever you ask in My name, that will I do, that the Father may be glorified in the Son. If you ask anything in My name, I will do it" (John 14:13–14). Whatever our request, it should glorify Jesus. That keeps us focused on things of God's kingdom, not for our own selfish gain. "You ask and do not receive, because you ask amiss, that you may spend it on your pleasures" (James 4:3). Sometimes, our prayers go unanswered because what we're asking for doesn't line up with God's will and Christ isn't glorified in our request.

Does this mean I shouldn't pray for God's blessings in my life?

Of course not! In *The Prayer of Jabez,* Wilkinson explains how Jabez prayed for God to bless him.[7] The Lord must have been pleased with his request because He answered him. Jabez asked for a supernatural favor with God, and he received it. If Jabez would have asked God to give him more "stuff" to impress his neighbors, his request wouldn't have been answered.

When we pray, we can talk to God about anything that concerns us. Martin Luther said, "We should pray for everything that tends to the glory of God and to our own and our neighbor's welfare, both spiritual and bodily blessings." [8]

Taking care of kingdom business is the reason we pray in Jesus' name. One example of kingdom business is teaching a Sunday school class. I discovered how much more powerfully I teach when I ask God to work through me. I want my students to experience what it means to live the Christian life, not just to learn Bible facts. I pray that God will use me to speak to their hearts, and that their lives will be changed. When I pray this way, I see results. That's the power behind praying in the name of Jesus.

I've found that whenever I ask God to help me with His work, and invite Him to work through me, He always does. Whenever I ask for a closer walk with Him, He gives me that, too. Anything I ask that has to do with kingdom business, God has answered. It seems as if He is not only willing, but anxious to answer such a request.

The seventh key: Come with a clean heart

> "Your iniquities have separated you from your God; and your sins have hidden His face from you, so that He will not hear."
>
> Isaiah 59:2

Sin cuts off our communion with God. We all sin daily, and that sin needs to be dealt with before God can hear our prayers.

> "If we say that we have no sin, we deceive ourselves, and the truth is not in us. If we confess our sins, He is faithful and just to forgive us our sins and to cleanse us from all unrighteousness. If we say that we have not sinned, we make Him a liar, and His word is not in us."
>
> 1 John 1:8–10

When we sin, we need to reconnect to God by confessing and forsaking everything that is wrong in our lives. Confess means to admit to God that we have done wrong. Then we need to ask God to help us overcome the temptation the next time. It does us no good to confess sin if we know we're going to do the same thing tomorrow.

After we confess our sin, we can then approach the throne of grace with confidence. "Let us therefore come boldly to the throne of grace, that we may obtain mercy and find grace to help in the time of need" (Hebrews 4:16). A clean heart makes us righteous; and "the effective, fervent prayer of a righteous man avails much" (James 5:16).

The eighth key: Come with a humble heart

Jesus told this parable to illustrate this point:

> "Two men went up to the temple to pray, one a Pharisee and the other a tax collector. The Pharisee stood and prayed thus with himself, 'God, I thank You that I am not like other men-extortionists, unjust adulterers, or even as this tax collector. I fast twice a week; I give tithes of all that I possess.' And the tax collector, standing afar off, would not so much as raise His eyes to heaven, but beat his breast saying, 'God, be merciful to me a sinner!' I tell you, this man went down to his house justified rather than the other, for everyone who exalts himself will be humbled, and he who humbles himself will be exalted."
>
> Luke 18:10–14

If we come before God thinking of how much better we are than other people, we're inviting destruction into our lives. King Solomon wrote, "Pride goes before destruction, and a haughty spirit before a fall" (Proverbs 16:18).

When we keep before us that we are sinners saved by unearned favor, we stay humble before God and men. We need to approach God as the tax collect did. We need to say, "Lord, have mercy on me, a sinner." Then, as Jesus said, we will be justified. That means "just as if I never sinned."

The ninth key: Come before God with a thankful heart

> "Be anxious for nothing, but in everything by prayer and supplication, with thanksgiving, let your request be made known to God; and the peace of God, which surpasses all understanding, will guard your hearts and minds through Christ Jesus,"
>
> Philippians 4:6–7

I like what Beth Moore says about the above verses in *Living Free:*

> "I decided that to bring home the impact of these verses, I would have a little fun and paraphrase the passage from a negative standpoint. In other words, I turned this prescription for peace into a no-fail prescription for anxiety. My result looked like this, 'Do not be calm about anything, but in everything, by dwelling on it constantly and feeling picked on by God, with thoughts like 'and this is the thanks I get,' present your aggravations to everyone you know but Him. And the acid in your stomach, which transcends all milk products, will cause you an ulcer, and the doctor bills will cause you a heart attack, and you will lose your mind." [9]

I like this because it demonstrates what happens when we don't take our request to God; but instead, worry and complain about our problems. Are you carrying a heavy burden? Perhaps you or your loved one got a bad report from the doctor. There might be a problem with your marriage, children, or job. None of us are exempt from trouble, no matter how close we are to God. He has promised to see us through our difficulties. We only need to bring our request to Him. We need to thank Him *in* the situation, not *for* the situation. As we praise and thank Him, He will work on our behalf to solve our difficulties. Most people complain to others about their problems. I often hear people talk about their spouses and other people. Instead of complaining about your spouse, neighbors, boss, or children, talk to God instead. "Cast your burden on the Lord, and He shall sustain you; He shall never permit the righteous to be moved" (Psalm 55:22).

I'm not suggesting that you never tell anyone about your difficulties. There are times we need to discuss a situation with a trusted friend, pastor or counselor. I'm referring to complaining about your spouse or gossiping about other people. "Do not speak evil of one another, brethren. He who speaks evil of a brother and judges his brother, speaks evil of the law and judges the law" (James 4:11). Rather than complain about our problems, we need to take them to God in prayer and leave them with Him.

The tenth key: Get rid of unbelief

"Let him ask in faith, with no doubting, for he who doubts is like a wave of the sea driven and tossed by the wind. For let not that man suppose that he will receive anything from the Lord; he is a double-minded man, unstable in all his ways" (James 1:6–8).

We can have faith that God can do what we ask for nothing is too difficult for Him. He can even do more than we can image. "Now to Him who is able to do exceedingly abundantly above all that we ask or think, according to the power that works in us" (Ephesians 3:20). That's a powerful verse. It means we never have to worry about asking for more than He's capable of doing, for nothing is too difficult for Him.

An example of this is in *Experiencing God,* by Henry Blackably.[10] He tells of believers in a certain church that felt God was leading them to open a medical clinic in their city. They knew it was God's will that they build the facility, but they lacked the funds. They prayed, and they were able to purchase a building within their budget. All the equipment they needed was then donated by a hospital that was closing. God provided all they needed. That was a big request, but it wasn't too big for God.

You can have confidence as you pray because you know God is able to do what you ask. In fact, when you pray in Jesus' name for kingdom business, and believe that He will do it, you might as well consider it done.

The eleventh key: Pray for the President and all who are in authority

> "I exhort first of all that supplication, prayers, intercessions, and giving of thanks be made for all men, for kings and all who are in authority, that we may lead a quiet and peaceable life in all godliness and reverence. For this is good and acceptable in the sight of God our Savior."
>
> I Timothy 2:1–3

Praying for our President and other leaders is far more important than most Christians realize. God's hand is moved to action when we intercede for our country. Paul tells us in 1 Timothy to pray *first* for all men, for kings and all those in authority. We're told to make supplication and intercession for them. Supplication is to pray earnestly. Little dinky one minute prayers won't do. The prayer that Catherine Marshall's mother prayed was intense and earnest. That's how we should pray for all those in authority over us. Intercession means to pray for someone who is in need. We're to stand in the gap, and give thanks for them. This includes not only the President, but those in congress, the Supreme Court, governors, mayors, the city council, police officers, pastors, and every one who has authority over us.

Most people don't realize the real problem in the world is in the spiritual realm. "For we do not wrestle against flesh and blood, but against principalities, against powers, against the rulers of the darkness of this age, against spiritual host of wickedness in the heavenly places" (Ephesians 6:12).

I understood this better after I read Frank Peretti's book, *This Present Darkness*.[11] This is a fictional story of a town that was taken over by evil. The action takes place on two plains—the spirit world and the natural world. Angels and demons fight against each other for control of the town.

The heroine of this story is an elderly woman who is a mighty prayer warrior. When she prays, angels are strengthened. Good prevails as long as she interceded. This is a fictional story, but it accurately portrays what is happening in the spiritual realm. It helped me understand how important prayer is in holding back the forces of evil that are attempting to take over America. The more Christians pray, the more God's hand is moved to change our world.

Once you become a prayer warrior, God will often waken you during the night to pray for a specific situation. You'll awake suddenly and fully alert. God could be calling you to pray for someone you know, or to intercede for our troops in harms way, or a crisis in Israel. If God awakens you suddenly during the night, ask Him to tell you what to pray about, and He will bring someone or some situation to your mind. God is looking for prayer warriors who can make a difference in people's lives and in our nation and the world.

He gives us this promise: "If My people who are called by My name will humble themselves, and pray and seek My face, and turn from their wicked ways, then I will hear from heaven, and will forgive their sins and heal their land" (2 Chronicles 7:14). This promise is for every nation.

If we want to see changes in our land, we must seek God's face, confess our sins, and pray for this nation. We must stop wasting time on trivial matters and get serious with God. Instead of watching television tonight, why not get down on your knees and pray for our country and its leaders? Also, pray for your state and local governments. Seek the face of God, and confess your sins before Him. We can turn back evil in this country if we continue to seek God's face.

God might place a particular burden on your heart to pray concerning our country. It could be the judicial system, our schools, the entertainment industry, or some other area. Whatever God places on your heart, pray much about that area. Then God will be attentive to your prayers. As you pray, the forces of darkness will be held back and you will see the hand of God moving. If every

Christian would intercede for some area in our country, this country would once again be a Christian nation.

This applies to all nations of the world, not just America. God desires that people in every nation come to Him. As believers in every country pray, they can affect their leaders, even those in Islamic or communist countries. If enough Christians pray, God's hand is moved to make changes.

Praying for those in authority also includes our pastors and other church leaders. Everyday I pray for our pastors and their families. They have tremendous responsibilities. Our pastors are responsible for our spiritual welfare. They feed us God's Word and shepherd us. It is in our best interest to pray for them so that they will be effective in their work. I had one pastor tell me he could feel the power of God in his life as a result of my intersession.

The time you spend talking to God is not wasted, for "the effective, fervent prayer of a righteous man avails much" James 5:16. All of us can bring positive changes to ourselves, our loved ones, and the nation by bringing petitions to God. Paul said in 1 Timothy to pray for all those in authority that we might live quiet, peaceful lives that are pleasing to God.

The twelfth key: Teach your children to pray

> "Train up a child in the way he should go, and when he is old he will not depart from it."
> Proverbs 22:6

It's our privilege and responsibility as parents and grandparents to pass spiritual truths to the next generation.

Catherine Marshall's mother taught her to pray, and it's a lesson that stayed with her for her entire life. As I read Catherine Marshall's autobiography, I was impressed by how often she prayed as an adult. This wouldn't have happened if her godly mother had not taught her.

If you're a parent, teaching your children to talk to God is one of the most important activities you can do. It's far more important that sports activities and music lessons. What your children learn about prayer will affect them not only in this life but in the next. When they leave this world, their eternal destiny is determined by their relationship with Christ; and that relationship begins and is enriched through prayer. So praying is one of the most important lessons you can teach them.

You must teach your children when they're young. It's more difficult with teenagers and impossible once they get out on their own. As you model how to talk to God, they'll listen and then do as you do.

The concept of God is difficult for young children to comprehend. They can, though, easily grasp the idea of answered prayer. When you talk to them about how God answered a particular prayer request, they'll discover that God is real and that He does hear and answer us. This will help them discover the nature and character of God. They'll learn that God cares about them and is able to meet their needs. Then when they have doubts about their faith, they will remember the many times God answered their prayer, and they'll *know* He exists.

You can ask God to protect your children before they go to school each day. Lay your hands on each child and pray for them before they leave in the morning. Schools used to be a safe place for children, but not any more.

In our world of school shootings and violence, you can ask God to watch over your children wherever they go. You can also pray for their teachers. As you pray for your children and their school, they will feel confident and secure as they leave home each morning.

Conclusion

These twelve keys are not the final word on prayer—the Bible has much more to say on this important subject. Unfortunately, they can't all be included in this chapter, but they're too important to omit. Therefore, I'm giving you the following Scripture verses to read and mediate on without making any commits on them. Not only are these verses worthy of our meditation, but also our memorization. Here they are:

Pray for the peace of Jerusalem: may they prosper who love you" (Psalm 122:6).

> "Love your enemies, bless those who curse you, do good to those who hate you, and pray for those who spitefully use you and persecute you, that you may be sons of your Father in heaven; for He makes His sun rise on the evil and on the good, and sends rain on the just and on the unjust."
> Matthew 5:44–45

> "When you pray, do not use vain repetitions as the heathen do. For they think that they will be heard for their many words."
> Matthew 6:7

"Then He said to His disciples, 'The harvest truly

is plentiful, but the laborers are few. Therefore pray the Lord of the harvest to send out laborers into His harvest."

Matthew 9:37–38

"Watch and pray, lest you enter into temptation."

Matthew 26:41

"Whenever you stand praying, if you have anything against anyone, forgive him, that your Father in heaven may also forgive your trespasses"."

Mark 11:25

"Then He spoke a parable to them, that men always ought to pray and not lose heart."

Luke 18:1

"Watch therefore, and pray always that you may be counted worthy to escape all these things that will come to pass, and to stand before the Son of Man."

Luke 21:36

"The righteous cry out, and the Lord hears, and delivers them out of all their troubles."

Psalm 34:17

Listening to God

We have spent this chapter discussing talking to God, but did you know that God speaks to us ever day—all day long? He speaks to us through our conscience, giving us direction as we go about the day. Unfortunately, most of us ignore His voice. We want to do our own thing. What blessings we miss by doing what we want rather than what God tells us to do. His ways are perfect. He tries to direct us in the best possible path, but we usually end up doing what we want and suffer the consequences.

I have found that God speaks to me most often during my quiet time each morning. He doesn't speak audibly, but He speaks through my mind. In fact, some of the content of this book has been brought to my mind during my prayer time. As I prayed, the Lord brought ideas for each chapter. I keep a pen and paper near by to write these down.

God will speak to you in the same way as you seek Him in prayer. He will also direct your path. Prayer is a two-way communication—you speak to God and the Holy Spirit speaks to you.

Now you have twelve keys that will help you unlock the blessings God has for you. Not only will you be blessed, but future generations will be also. And our nation and world will be affected your prayers. When you pray for our government and other vital issues, you can make a difference. You and I have the power through prayer to change the world.

Endnotes

1. Catherine Marshall. Meeting God at Every Turn (Carmel, NY: Guidepost, 1980).
2. Fredrick K. C. Price. The Word Study Bible (Tulsa, OK: Harrison House, 1990), p. 1177.

3. Madame Guyon. Experiencing God through Prayer (New Kensington, PA: Whitaker House, 1984) p.17.
4. E. M. Bounds. The Complete Works of E. M. Bounds on Prayer (Grand Rapids, Michigan: Baker House, 1990, 118.
5. E. M. Bound. Complete Works, 120.
6. Ruth Ward Heflin. Glory (Hagerstown, MD: McDougal Publishing, 1999).
7. Bruce H. Wilkinson. The Prayer of Jabez (Sisters, OR: Multnomah Publishers, 2000.
8. Martin Luther. Luther's Small Catechism. (St. Louis, Missouri: Concordia Publishing House, 1971), 147.
9. Beth Moore. Living Free (Nashville: LifeWay Press, 2001), 83.
10. Henry T. Blackaby & Claude V. King. Experiencing God (Nashville, TN: The Sunday School Board of the Southern Baptist Convention, 1990).
11. Kenneth E. Hagin. The Art of Prayer (Tulsa, OK: Rhema Bible Church, 1998), p. 143–145.
12. Frank Peretti. This Present Darkness (Wheaton, IL: Crossway Books, 1986).

The Glorious Church— The Bride of Christ

- "Who needs the church? I can worship God just as well at home."
- "I want to join a church, but how do I find the right one?"
- "I used to go to services almost every Sunday. Then I got sick and no one visited me in the hospital. I haven't been back since."
- "Sure, I'm a member of a church, but I don't go very often. I just don't get anything out of the services."
- "Are groups like the Mormons and Jehovah Witnesses really saved?"
- "I had too much of the church when I was growing up. I don't need it now."

Would you know how to respond if someone asked you about these topics? Or perhaps some of these express your own thoughts. These are important issues that affect our lives now and our eternal destiny. In this chapter, we'll discuss each of these from a biblical point of view. Let's start with the matter of church membership.

Can't I be a Christian without joining a church?

Yes you can, but you won't be as effective. Joining a church never saved anyone; our salvation is through faith in Christ, but being a church member has many benefits, as we'll see throughout this chapter. If you want to live triumphantly, you must stay connected to the local body of believers. Can you name one Christian who has accomplished something for God that wasn't connected to a local church? That's the only way to stay strong in your faith and be at your best spiritually.

Why is the Church referred to as the body of Christ and also the Bride of Christ?

God wanted us to understand the Church and its functions. He gave us these word pictures to help us. The Church is referred to in the Scripture as the Bride of Christ. God's purpose for the Church is to have an eternal Bride for His Son. I like the way Paul Billheimer describes the Bride of Christ in his book, *Destined for the Throne,* page 22.

> "The human race was created in the image and likeness of God for one purpose: to provide an eternal companion for the Son. After the fall and promise of redemption through the coming Messiah, the Messianic race was born and nurtured in order to bring in the Messiah. And the Messiah came for one intent and only one: to give birth to His Church, thus to obtain His Bride. The Church then, the called-out body of redeemed mankind—turns out to be the central object, the goal, not only of mundane history

but of all that God has been doing in all realms from all eternity."

From this, we see that the purpose of the Church is to have an eternal Bride for Christ, who will rule and reign with Him in the age to come. Each time we attend a Christian wedding, we're reminded that marriage represents the union between Christ and the Church.

The Church is also referred to as a body and Christ is its head. This body is made up of all true born-again Christians from every language, tribe and nation. (This universal Church is spelled with a capital C.) Not everyone who is a church member is a member of Christ's body. Only those who have put their faith in Christ make up the universal Church. Some people come to services to impress others or to appear religious. Or they might come only for socialization. These people are not part of the true Church. All born again believers who haven't joined a local congregation are also part of the Church.

Being a member of a Bible-believing church helps believers grow strong in the Lord. This is a life-long process; we never become so spiritual that we out-grow our need for the church. A person who doesn't belong to a church is like a sheep that has strayed from the fold. He's vulnerable to attack from wolfs. He remains safe only as long as he stays under the shepherd's care.

People who are shut-ins and elderly still benefit from being connected to the church even when they can no longer attend services. These seasoned saints know how to accomplish much by their intercessory prayer. They can also encourage others by making phone calls and sending cards. The pastor and others from the church visit with them and help with spiritual needs. They're still connected to the body. Being connected to the church helps all believers grow in their faith.

If there's only one true Church, why are there so many denominations?

Even though we are all one body, the Church is made up of various denominations. They have slightly different beliefs, but one thing is certain—each holds that the Bible is God's Word and that salvation is by faith in Christ. All true churches accept these as fact. Christians call themselves by different names such as Presbyterian, Lutherans, or Methodist, but we are all part of Christ's body.

Until the Reformation in the sixteenth century, there were only the Roman Catholic and the Greek Orthodox churches. Oh, there were some dissenters, such as the Anti-Baptist, who rejected infant baptism in favor of believers' baptism; but there were no organized denominations as we know them today. Then in the 1500's, Martin Luther began to bring the Bible back to the Roman Catholic Church. The Church at that time was selling indulgences, where people were led to believe they could buy their way to heaven. Martin Luther proclaimed that salvation is by faith in Christ, not by indulgences. The result was the Reformation, and the founding of the Lutheran Church. From the Lutheran Church, other sects sprang up.

Today, we have several mainline denominations. They don't agree on some issues such as how to baptize and how often to administer the Lord's Supper. They might differ in the way they interpret some Scripture, but they all agree that Jesus is the Son of God, and it's through faith in Him alone that we have salvation. Also, they agree that the Bible is the inspired Word of God. These two vital issues—faith in Christ alone for salvation and the Bible as the Word of God—are the bases of the Church.

Does that mean that it doesn't matter which church I join since they're all alike?

As you look for a church, you'll find a variety of churches within each denomination. Some are more liberal than others. For example, many, but not all, United Methodist churches now preach a social gospel. (There's more about the social gospel in the next paragraph.) Some United Methodist churches still preach salvation by faith. There're even a few that are charismatic, with all the gifts of the Spirit in use. This is not only true of United Methodist churches, many denominations fall into this category. You'll find a wide variety of churches in all denominations.

Unfortunately, some churches no longer believe the Bible is the inspired Word of God and that salvation is by faith in Christ. How could this happen? Although there have always been a few churches that have rejected salvation by faith, a large-scale departure from the fundamentals of Christianity began about a hundred years ago with the invention of a social gospel, which teaches salvation by doing good works.

This social gospel comes from the unholy trinity, consisting of Satan, the world, and the flesh. Paul tells us that this will happen before Christ returns. "In latter times some will depart from the faith, giving heed to deceiving spirits and doctrines of demons, speaking lies in hypocrisy, having their own conscience seared with a hot iron" (1 Timothy 4:1–2). Satan has filled some people's hearts to destroy the church; and they're doing it from within. Men and woman have infiltrated churches in various denominations who claim to be Christians, but they are motivated by the dark forces of evil. These people hold key positions in the governing bodies of many churches. They are pastors, bishops and teachers. Whatever their title, their mission is the same: to take away the effectiveness of the body of Christ.

They have deceived many into believing that the Bible is not the inspired inerrant Word of God. They have a way of explaining the miracles in the Scriptures. For example, they say that the crossing of the Red Sea wasn't a miracle. Their explanation is that the Israelites crossed the Red Sea during the dry season, so of course they went across on dry land. (They don't have an explanation of how the entire Egyptian army drowned on dry land!) They also try to convince people that the virgin birth never occurred. These erroneous doctrines are further promoted through television programs, movies, and books.

The most dangerous lie they have is to convince the church that people don't need to be saved. The redeeming power of the blood of Jesus has been replaced with their social gospel of salvation by good works. Their doctrine is to do well to your neighbor, and you will earn your way to heaven. They never teach or even sing about the blood of Jesus. Hymns such as "The Old Rugged Cross" are no longer in their hymn books. The devil knows there is power in the Word of God, blood of Jesus, and in the name of Jesus. He wants to keep the church from knowing about and using this power.

They will do anything to keep you from knowing that there is only one way to heaven, and that is by the way of the cross. You must believe that Jesus died to take away your sins. There's no other way to eternal life, no matter what any pastor or Bible teacher says.

Are Roman Catholics part of the true Church?

They are if they have placed their faith in Christ. That alone is the only way of eternal life. "If you confess with your mouth the Lord Jesus and believe in your heart that God has raised Him from the dead, you will be saved. For with the heart one believes unto righteousness, and with the mouth confession is made unto salvation" (Romans 10:9–10). Paul makes clear that works are not part of salvation. "For by grace you have been saved through faith, and that not of yourselves; it is the gift of God, not of works, lest anyone should boast" (Ephesians 2:8–9). According to the Bible, baptism, Eucharist, and good works never got anyone to heaven. I have known many devout Catholics that I believe are saved, and if they are, it is by faith in Christ alone.

What about groups such as Jehovah Witnesses, Mormons, and Christian Scientists?

Some groups that call themselves Christians have doctrines far from what the Bible teaches. These groups are referred to as cults rather than churches. Examples of these are Jehovah Witnesses, Christian Scientist, and the Church of Jesus Christ of the Latter Day Saints, better known as the Mormons. Each of these denies that Jesus is the only begotten Son of God and that salvation is by faith in Christ alone. They each have additional writings that supersede the Bible. (The Jehovah Witnesses have their own version of the Bible, which they have modified to fit their beliefs.) These groups might claim to teach faith in Christ alone for salvation, but if you exam their actual doctrine, you'll find they don't. If you're considering joining one of these cults, I would suggest you read Josh McDowell's book, *The Deceivers,* by Here's Life Publishers. 1992. He explains what each of these cults actually believe, and how their beliefs differ from the Bible.

These groups teach that there is some other way to be saved other than by faith in Christ. There is only one plan of salvation, though, and Jesus paid a high price for it. The night before He was crucified, Christ asked His Father if there was any other way for mankind to be redeemed. Then He prayed, "Not as I will, but as You will" (Matthew 26:39). If there had been another way of salvation, God would have spared His dear Son, but there wasn't. Jesus had to die for our sins. It is only by the shed blood of Jesus that we can find forgiveness of our sins and have a right standing with God. Paul said, "If we, or an angel from heaven, preach any other gospel to you than what we have preached to you, let him be accursed" (Galatians 1:8).

It isn't just from cults that we need to be on guard. Beware of any pastor or Bible teacher of any denomination who doesn't hold to what the Bible teaches. Just because someone has the title of pastor or teacher doesn't automatically mean that they have sound doctrine.

Many people have been led astray by false teachers and preachers.

Pastors and church leaders need to be filled with the Spirit. They should be men and women of integrity who love the Lord and serve Him faithfully. Jesus had harsh words for religious leaders who only had the appearance of righteousness. "Woe to you, scribes and Pharisees, hypocrites! For you are like whitewashed tombs which indeed appear beautiful outwardly, but inside are full of dead men's bones and all uncleanness" (Matthew 23:27). You don't want a church filled with "dead men's bones," but rather is alive with God's Spirit.

How can I keep from being deceived by any church, cult or person?

I once heard that people who study counterfeit currency examine only genuine money. They spend so much time looking at the real thing that they can easily spot anything phony. We can use this same reasoning to find a genuine church. The Bible is our standard for determining what is authentic. We can find an example of a true church at the end of the second chapter of Acts. Let's dig into these verses. We'll discover how to distinguish a genuine church from one that's counterfeit.

The Jerusalem church is a paradigm of what every place of worship should be. What they did is an example for us. Luke, the writer of the book of Acts, says,

> "They continued steadfastly in the apostles' doctrine and fellowship, in the breaking of bread, and in prayers. Then fear came upon every soul, and many wonders and signs were done through the apostles.

> Now all who believed were together, and had all things in common, and sold their possessions and goods, and divided them among all, as anyone had need. So continuing daily with one accord in the temple, and breaking bread from house to house, they ate their food with gladness and simplicity of heart, praising God, and having favor with all the people. And the Lord added to the church daily those who were being saved."
>
> Acts 2:42–47

These verses contain ten essential elements that should be in every church. Let's take a closer look at each of these. Any congregation you're considering joining or are now a member of, should be like the Jerusalem church.

1. "They continued steadfastly in the apostles' doctrine" Acts 2:42. The apostles were the twelve who were with Jesus during His earthly ministry. They learned from Him first-hand and then they taught the Jerusalem believers.

Today, the mark of a genuine church is that it regards the Bible as the inerrant Word of God. I like what *The Baptist Faith and Message* says on this subject.

> "The Holy Bible was written by men divinely inspired and is God's revelation of Himself to man. It is a perfect treasure of divine instruction. It has God for its author, salvation for its end, and truth, without any mixture of error, for its matter."

A genuine church will hold to what the Bible teaches.

Teaching the Scriptures to believers is a vital function of the church. Christians grow through sermons, the Sunday school, and Bible study groups. Every able-bodied church member should be involved in some type of discipleship. As we've seen earlier in this chapter, not all churches believe the Bible to be the inspired Word of God. You'll need to find one that does.

2. The church also broke bread together. This refers to what we call communion, Eucharist, or the Lord's Supper. Paul tells us,

> "The Lord Jesus on the same night in which He was betrayed took bread; and when He had given thanks, He broke it and said, 'Take, eat, this is My body which is broken for you; do this in remembrance of Me.' In the same manner He also took the cup after supper, saying, 'This cup is the new covenant in My blood. This do, as often as you drink it, in remembrance of Me.' For as often as you eat this bread and drink this cup, you proclaim the Lord's death till He comes."
>
> 1 Corinthians 11:23–26

Taking the Lord's Supper is a holy occasion in the church. We remember at that time the sacrifice that Jesus made for us. This should be a solemn and soul-searching experience. Pastors should remind the congregation of Paul's warning,

> "Whoever eats this bread or drinks this cup of the Lord in an unworthy manner will be guilty of the

body and the blood of the Lord. But let a man examine himself, and so let him eat of the bread and drink of the cup. For he who eats and drinks in an unworthy manner eats and drinks judgment to himself, not discerning the Lord's body. For this reason many are weak and sick among you, and many sleep. For if we would judge ourselves, we would not be judged."

1 Corinthians 11:27–31

Christ gave us the Lord's Supper to keep His sacrifice fresh in our minds. We are to come to His table remembering His suffering. We should then search our hearts for any unconfessed sin. It's better to refuse the Lord's Supper than to take it unworthily. As we're taking communion and thinking of Christ's death, it's a good time to make a renewed commitment to Him.

3. The Jerusalem church also prayed together. Jesus said, "My house shall be called a House of Prayer" (Matthew 21:13). Prayer is a vital link to every ministry of the church. Pastors need to pray about their sermons and listen to what God speaks into their spirit. Teachers should pray over their lessons. The success of every program of the church is dependent on prayer. The power of a praying church extends beyond its doors to affect our city, state, nation, and world. Unfortunately, many churches are powerless because they are prayerless.

What would happen if our churches today were really houses of prayer? If Christians would gather together, confess their sins and sincerely seek God's face, God would be unleashed to do great miracles. The Holy Spirit would be poured out among the people. Revival would come. And God would heal those sick in body and spirit. He would also heal our land. America would be turned back to God if enough churches truly were houses of prayer.

Our church needs to be a house of prayer, but I don't know how to get people motivated to pray. What can we do?

Jesus said you have not because you ask not. Diligently seek His face and ask Him to show you how your church can become a house of prayer. After you pray, listen to what the Holy Spirit speaks to your spirit. God knows exactly what will work in your particular church, and He desires for it to be done. It's prayers such as this that God delights in answering. I've found every time I ask God for wisdom in doing something that will further His kingdom, He's more that anxious to do it. This is the kind of prayer God is waiting for us to pray.

We can pray at home about problems facing our nation, but our individual prayers are not strong enough to accomplish what we ask. "For we do not wrestle against flesh and blood, but against principalities, against powers, against the rulers of the darkness of this age, against spiritual hosts of wickedness in the heavenly places" (Ephesians 6:12). These evil forces are powerful and numerous. They are defeated only when many people join together to pray.

An example of this happened in Columbus, Ohio. A sniper terrorized the south side, shooting at cars driving along a freeway. One woman was killed and many cars were shot at. This went on for several months. Many people prayed that the sniper would be caught, but the shootings continued. The police had no leads in this case. Then a pastor called for a city-wide prayer meeting. Within one or two days, the shooter's identity was known. A few days later, he was captured. This illustrates the power of people banding together to pray. God desires that our churches truly be houses of prayer. He's waiting anxious to bless us when this happens.

4. "Many wonders and signs were done through the apostles" (Acts 2:43). The apostles preformed many miracles just as Jesus had done. Actually, it was the Holy Spirit working through them. The book of Acts records several healings that God did through the Apostles. These miracles weren't just for the first century believers. Everything the Jerusalem church did was done as an example for us. Miracles are taking place in many churches around the world. In fact, I see so many people healed and lives changed at Evangel Temple that miracles now seem common place to me.

Recently, we had a healing service at our church, and there was a real manifest presence of God. That Sunday night service had almost as many people as we normally have on Sunday mornings. All those who needed prayer formed two lines, one for healing; and another for any other need. Our pastors anointed each person with oil, laid hands on them, and prayed. Many people were healed in this service. It's God's desire to make His people whole, and when He's given the opportunity, He'll do it. Not everyone goes away healed in these services, but many are. This is awesome to witness. I get excited when I see miracles done as they were in the New Testament church. You can find healing services such as this in many denominations around the world. God hasn't changed; He's still in the miracle-working business today.

5. The church had all things in common and they divided their possessions among those in need. Today, we don't have all things in common as they did, but we still are helping those in need. The local church is one body of believers. When part of the body hurts, we all should feel the pain. This was made clear to me when some friends of ours had a seven-year-old son who developed a rare form of cancer. They belong to a large church in Atlanta. Members of their church cleaned their house, brought meals and watched the other children while the father worked and the mother stayed at the hospital. That church is one body that stands together when one of its families faces a crisis.

When Jesus was on earth, He fed the hungry and tended to the needs of the poor. He's no longer here in bodily form; we are His body, and it's our responsibly to do as He did. This includes feeding the hungry, providing clothing or other assistance to those in need. Jesus said, "Inasmuch as you did it to one of the least of these My brethren, you did it to Me" (Matthew 25:40). All denominations are involved in some type of outreach to those in need. This is one area where churches in a neighborhood could work together to help the needy in their community.

6. This leads to the next element—they had unity. The Jerusalem church met together regularly. They had unity in their beliefs, holding to the teachings of the apostles and they agreed on matters in the church. Not only did they have unity of doctrine, they were one body, united in love.

Today, many churches are filled with grumbling people. They gossip and complain about many issues. This lessens the effectiveness of the congregation. We should over look and forgive minor offenses. Major difficulties need to be handled according to Scripture. Members need to seek unity and love each other.

7. The Jerusalem church also ate and fellowshipped together. Churches today have social activities. These might seem insignificant, but those pot luck dinners and Christmas parties are an important part of the church. It's from these activities that you get to know others in the congregation. Friendships are formed. People are helped. But most important, we form bonds that help us love each other. Jesus said, "By this all will know that you are My disciples, if you have love for one another" (John 13:35). Genuine love comes from knowing each other, and you can't really know someone by seeing them only on Sunday mornings.

Does this mean that I have to love everybody at church?

When you're a member of a church, you can be sure that someone will offend you. They might gossip about you; not speak to you, or (heaven forbid) the pastor might fail to visit you when you're in the hospital. Whatever it is, someone will hurt your feelings. You could get angry and stop attending services, or find another church. Then when you find a new one, someone there will eventually offend you. You could go from church to church every time someone makes you anger. Or you could just deal with the hurt or resentment, and forgive them. After all, we're all guilty of hurting other people. Think of the times you have hurt others. Then think of the many times God has forgiven you. If you want Him to forgive you, you need to forgive others of the wrong they have done to you.

Matthew tells us, "Peter came to Him and said, 'Lord, how often shall my brother sin against me, and I forgive him? Up to seven times?' Jesus said to him, 'I do not say to you up to seven times, but up to seventy times seven" (Matthew 18:21–22).

Our eyes should be on Jesus, not on other people in the church. People will disappoint us: Jesus never will. I've seen members leave a church when the pastor leaves. That indicates that their focus wasn't on Christ, but the preacher. If we keep our heart on Him rather than on anyone else, we won't be shaken.

Perhaps the church you attend has a problem and you feel like leaving. If you leave and join another congregation, you'll find that one also has problems. There's no perfect church. Churches are made up of people and we all make mistakes. Does that mean you should give up attending services? The Scriptures tells us, "Not forsaking the assembling of ourselves together, as is the manner of some, but exhorting one another, and so much the more as you see the Day approaching" (Hebrews 10:25). You need the church and the church needs you, even though neither is perfect.

8. They also praised God. Another important function of a church is to worship. Our church services should actually be a worship service, with a real emphasizes on worship. We should come to church with the desire to worship God. And we should come joyfully. The Psalmist tells us, "Enter into His gates with thanksgiving, and into His courts with praise. Be thankful to Him, and bless His name."

Psalm 100:4

We need to worship in spirit and in truth. To worship in spirit means to worship with our spirit. God is a spirit, and our spirit connects with His as we worship Him. The word truth in this verse comes from the Greek word *alethinos,* which means ideal or genuine. God is seeking people who genuinely worship Him with their spirits. And it's those people He pours out His blessings upon.

The Psalmist tells us how to worship:

"Oh come, let us sing to the Lord! Let us shout joyfully to the Rock of our salvation. Let us come before His presence with thanksgiving; let us shout joyfully to Him with psalms. For the Lord is the great God, and the great King above all gods."

Psalm 95:1–3

When we sing, we are not just singing a song, but singing *to Him.* You can sing traditional hymns or modern choruses. It doesn't matter how well you sing. Even if you're like me and can't carry a tune, you can still praise God with a song. There is something about singing that stirs God's heart.

9. The Jerusalem church found favor with all people. It's not surprising that churches find favor the same way today. Christians do a lot of good in the community. They reach out to those in need. Church members generally are moral, compassionate people who carry on the work of Christ. There are some exceptions to this, and those are the ones that get media attention; but the vast majority of Christians are law-biding citizens who quietly do much good in their community. They are the salt of the earth and light of the world. No wonder Christians find favor with God and man.

10. "The Lord added to the church daily those who were being saved" (Acts 2:47). One of the most important functions of the church is evangelism. In every worship service, the plan of salvation should be clearly stated, and people should be given an opportunity to respond. There might be unsaved people present, and they should be told how to accept Christ. The way of salvation should be explained plainly and simply. No pastor should ever assume that every person present is a Christian.

The church is to take the gospel to the world. That's the charge Jesus gave His followers before He returned to heaven. "Go therefore and make disciples of all the nations, baptizing them in the name of the Father and of the Son and of the Holy Spirit" (Matthew 28:19).

For the church, this means sending out missionaries to other countries and here at home. All mainline denominations that I'm aware of have missionaries around the world, but evangelism doesn't stop there. The message of salvation should be taken to those in the community. But it isn't just the pastor's job to evangelize—that's the responsibly of every church member. We all need to be involved in personal one-on-one witnessing of our faith. Now I know that we can't bring one soul into the kingdom of God—that's the work of the Holy Spirit, but He does work through us if we are willing.

Wait a minute! Don't expect me to tell people about Jesus. That makes me nervous. Besides, I don't know what to say.

Talking to people about the Lord is difficult for most of us. We don't want to offend anyone, and often Christians don't know what to say. But Jesus didn't make witnessing optional. We're all commanded to take the gospel to our neighbors. When we consider that every person who dies without accepting Christ as Savior will spend eternity in hell, it makes us realize how important it is to tell everyone we meet about Jesus. We need to see the lost the way Christ sees them. He loved them enough to suffer and die in their place. Shouldn't we love them enough to tell them about Him?

When we have a burden for the lost the way Jesus does, we'll make an effort to bring them to the Lord. We'll learn how to witness in the power of the Holy Spirit and overcome the nervousness we have and focus our attention upon those who are on their way to eternal separation from God. Let's take a look at the steps we need to take to lead someone to faith in Christ.

First, we can't bring anyone to salvation—that's the work of the Holy Spirit. No one comes to Christ unless the Spirit draws them, but the Holy Spirit works through us if we're willing to be used. But God will only use a clean vessel. It isn't the length of time you've been a Christian; it's how dedicated and obedient you are to Him.

If you want to lead others to faith in Christ, begin by asking God to bring people to you who are seeking Him. Ask for boldness and the right words to say. Then God will place people in your path who are searching for Him. Whatever conversation you have, turn it some how to spiritual matters. Then say something like, "If you died tonight, would you know for sure that you'd go to heaven?"

You can explain that we've all broken the Ten Commandments and deserve eternal punishment. But Jesus took the punishment we deserve. If we place our faith in Him, we can have eternal life.

When you lead someone to faith in Christ, they'll be grateful for what you've done. This isn't the only reward you'll receive for your effort. There's also a crown of rejoicing for all soul winners.

Not every one you witness to will place their faith in Christ, but don't be discouraged. God rewards obedience. Remember, you might sow the seed of salvation. Later someone else waters it, and then another person reaps the harvest; and you all will share in the reward.

I'm thankful to have spent many years as a Southern Baptist. The church I attended instructed me how to witness to others. Now I find it easy to talk to people about their need of salvation, but this wouldn't have happened if I would not have been taught.

Training members how to bring others into God's kingdom is not just for one denomination, or church leaders. All churches should have classes periodically on how to evangelize. People need to be taught how to go out into the community, and in the power of the Holy Spirit, tell people how to be saved. This is one of the most important functions of the church, and without it, the church isn't fulfilling its mission to reach the lost.

One indication of a genuine church is not how many people join from other congregations or how many children were baptized. The mark of a genuine church is how many lost people came to place their faith in Christ. Many congregations go for an entire year without reaching even one lost person. If the church you attend falls in this category, it's time to make a change.

What do I do once I join a church?

Be more than a "Sunday morning Christian." That refers to someone who attends only on Sunday mornings; they're never present at other services. These people sit in a pew once a week and do nothing. Let's discover what they're missing.

The church isn't a building; the church is a body of believers. Every member is part of a living organism; not merely an organization, and every person is significant. That's because we each have been given spiritual gifts and talents to be used in the church. These are to benefit the entire body. Examples of talents are singing and playing a musical instrument. Spiritual gifts include preaching and teaching. The Holy Spirit gives each believer at least one spiritual gift. Spiritual gifts and talents are vital to the body of Christ. Those who don't use their gifts affect the functioning of the entire body. It's like trying to get along without your right hand or left foot.

When I joined a new church several years ago, I wasn't involved in any type of ministry for a short time. My spiritual gift is teaching, but I wasn't using it; and I felt miserable. How much more content I was when I began teaching Sunday school. Using my gift not only affected me at church, but it affected my entire well-being. I believe not using our spiritual gifts and talents is the root cause of depression for some people. God gave us these gifts to be used, not ignored.

Many Christians are missing out on God's blessings, and they're also depriving the church of their gift. If all those "Sunday morning Christians" would become participating members, image how much better the church would function. Every Sunday school class would have adequate teachers. All services would have enough musicians, both vocal and instrumental. There would be enough nursery workers. New people would be added to the body regularly. Additional ministries would be started; and as a result, the community, city, state, nation, and the entire world would be impacted. Paul said in Ephesians, "The whole body, joined, and knit together by what every joint supplies, according to the effective working by which every part does its share, causes growth of the body for the edifying of itself in love" (Ephesians 4:16).

But I don't have any talents to use in the church

Yes you do! The Holy Spirit gives at least one spiritual gift to every believer. You might not have discovered yours yet, but you can. Jesus said, "Seek and you will find; knock, and it will be opened to you" (Luke 11:9). Just pray and ask God to show you what He wants you to do. If you're a clean vessel, He'll place something on your heart that needs to be done; and it will require using the gifts you have. That will be the area where He wants you to work.

If you're an active member of a Bible-believing church—good for you! If you're a new Christian, or one who is searching for a church, I hope what you've read will help you find the right one.

If you're still confused about this matter, here's some additional help. As I was thinking on this subject, I imaged what Jesus would tell someone who is looking for a church. Here it is what I believe He would say:

> "My dear child, I am the Good Shepherd. I have but one flock. My sheep can be found in every church. They hear my voice and follow Me. They love Me and obey Me. I am not so concerned with what church you belong to, but rather that you belong to Me. There are those in every church who are my sheep, and some who are not mine. Those who are mine love Me and keep My commandments.

> "Remember that denominations are man-made. My Church is universal. Look at the nail scares in my hands. I suffered and died for the whole world, not just for one denomination. When I see churches

competing against each other, I want to show them my hands, and remind them that My blood was shed for everyone. I love you all and I want you to love one another. While I was on the earth, I prayed to My Father that My sheep would be one, just as the Father and I are one. I want them to have one mind, guided by the Holy Spirit. I do not favor one denomination over another.

"If you are wondering about which church to join, remember that I will be with you as you make your choice. Seek My face and direction. Know this: the steps of a righteous man or woman are guided by Me. I will guide you to the place where your particular gifts and talents are needed. When you find the right church, you will have peace. Remember that I love you, and I will never leave you."

Love, Jesus

Endnotes

1. Billheimer, Paul E, Destined for the Throne (Fort Washington, Pa: Christian Literature Crusade, 1975) page 22.

Builders in the Kingdom

You've been invited into the construction business, working along side Christ as He builds His church. This construction is going on now, and He needs our help. Like any apprentice, we need to learn the tools of our trade. That's what we'll discover in this chapter.

Each of us has been given an important job in the construction of the church. Some are pastors and teachers; others are gifted in music or other areas. You've been given a job, too—even if you haven't discovered yours yet. These jobs are to build the church that the gates of hell cannot prevail against. And like any construction job, you need proper tools to complete the task. Let's find out what those tools are.

Grab your hammer, and let's get going. We have a lot of ground to cover. Since this terrain might be unfamiliar to you, I'm asking that you bring along some extra supplies. The first is an open mind. Some of this material probably will challenge your beliefs, but stick with me. Everything you're about to read is strictly from the Scripture. Also bring along the Holy Spirit who will guide you into all truth. In fact, why don't you invite Him to take this journey with you?

"Dear Holy Spirit, I'm like a little child when it comes to understanding Your mighty works. Open my eyes and my heart to what You want to teach me."

If you're ready, let's go!

As we arrive at the job site, we find that the foundation has already been laid. The foundation of the church is Jesus Christ himself. Paul tells us in 1 Corinthians,

> "According to the grace of God which was given to me, as a wise master builder I have laid the foundation, and another builds on it. But let each one take heed how he builds on it. For no other foundation can anyone lay than that which is laid, which is Jesus Christ."
>
> 1 Corinthians 3:10–11

The foundation of the Church is Jesus Christ. It is through His death and resurrection that the Church was established. From this foundation all of our work will be done. We will not work alone for the Holy Spirit will work along with us.

To help us do our work, God has given us special tools. These are the gifts of the Spirit. There are about twenty-two gifts that are mentioned throughout the New Testament, and this might not be the total number. A spiritual gift must edify and build ministry. Paul explains in Ephesians the purpose of these gifts, "He Himself gave some to be apostles, some prophets, some evangelists, and some pastors and teachers, for the equipping of the saints for the work of ministry, for the edifying of the body of Christ" (Ephesians 4:11–12).

There are nine manifestation gifts mentioned in 1 Corinthians 12:8–10. These are: the word of wisdom, the word of knowledge, faith, gifts of healing, working of miracles, prophecy, discerning of spirits, different kinds of tongues, and interpretation of tongues. These gifts are given by the Holy Spirit to believers as He chooses. They are to benefit the entire church. "There are diversities of gifts, but the same Spirit. There are differences of ministries, but the same Lord. And there are diversities of activities, but it is the same God who works all in all. But the manifestation of the Spirit is given to each one for the profit of all" (1 Corinthians 12:4–7).

But wait! As we get closer to the job sight, we find that not all the workers have their tools. There seems to be a disagreement among the laborers about what tools to use. Let's listen to what some of them are saying.

"Not all of the gifts of the Spirit are for today's church," one says. "Some ended after the apostolic age, that is, when the apostles died."

"Not so," says one of the other workers. "We're using all of the gifts of the Spirit. They're in operation today, just as they were in the first century. These gifts give us power and boldness to do God's work effectively."

So there is a problem among the workers. Some say the gifts of healing, prophecy, miracles, and tongues are not for today's church. How do we settle this labor dispute? Whenever there's a disagreement among workers, it's best to go to the management for the boss's opinion. In this case, we'll consult the Workers' Manual, the Bible, written by the Manager Himself. We'll find out what He has to say about this matter.

It appears as if this dispute has arisen because of a misinterpretation of Paul's first letter to the Corinthians. Paul wrote,

> "Love never fails. But whether there are prophecies, they will fail; whether there are tongues, they will cease; whether there is knowledge, it will vanish away; for we know in part and we prophesy in part. But when that which is perfect has come, then that which is in part will be done away."
>
> 1 Corinthians 13:8–10

When Paul said, "When that which is perfect has come, then that which is in part shall be done away" refers to the end of the present Church age. The gifts of the Spirit will not be needed in heaven; therefore, they will cease—when that which is perfect has come. All the spiritual gifts are needed by the church until then. Without them, the church is not operating at top efficiency.

This disagreement about some of the gifts of the Spirit has caused difficulty among Christians. I believe that many believers know in their hearts that these gifts are intended to be used until Christ returns; but because these gifts have been misused or misunderstood at times, they don't want to deal with it. In doing this, they rob themselves of the full power of the Holy Spirit, and the use of valuable tools intended for the ministry. Sometimes, there have been angry and harsh words spoken on both sides. Sometimes, both sides have forgotten to show love for each other.

Paul tells us that love is greater than all spiritual gifts.

"Though I speak with the tongues of men and of angels, but have not love, I have become sounding brass or a clanging cymbal. And though I have the gift of prophecy, and understand all mysteries and all knowledge, and though I have all faith, so that I could remove mountains, but have not love, I am nothing."

1 Corinthians 13:1–2

Perhaps if Christians would consider these verses, they would be able to work through their disagreements and work together to build God's kingdom—no matter how they felt about the matter of tongues and other gifts. Jesus said to love one another as I have loved you. No matter how you feel about this issue, if you are a child of God, you need to love your fellow Christians who disagree with you.

If you believe that speaking in tongues ended with the Apostles, then this chapter and the next aren't for you. You can skip these and go directly to chapter seven, dealing with spiritual warfare. These two chapters are written to those who desire to know more about the baptism of the Holy Spirit and help those who have received this gift have a better understanding of how the manifestation gifts work.

If these gifts of the Spirit are for today's church, how do I get them? I don't see them used in any church I've attended.

Just as a contractor wouldn't give a powerful tool to someone hired in off the street, so the manifestation gifts aren't given automatically when we're saved. They are given to those who are serious builders in God's kingdom. (There's more about these gifts in the next chapter.) These are intended for every believer because every believer has a job in building God's kingdom. Not every Christian, though, desires to be a builder. As a general rule, you have to ask for these tools. Sometimes, though, the Holy Spirit gives these gifts without asking. An example of this is Cornelius and his household. Everyone present received the baptism of the Holy Spirit without even knowing that such an experience existed. (See Acts 10.) The same thing can happen today, although this is not how most people receive this gift.

I was baptized in water. Does that mean I have the baptism of the Holy Spirit?

No, this is a separate experience. Water baptism takes place when you come into God's family. All believers are commanded to be baptized in water. The baptism of the Holy Spirit is a separate experience and involves being completely filled with the Spirit. (Some people receive this gift at the time of their salvation, but even then it's a separate occurrence. This is also referred to as the second blessing, or being full of the Holy Spirit. The most common term is baptism of the Holy Spirit. It makes no difference what you call this experience.

Jesus mentioned both water baptism and the baptism of the Holy Spirit before He returned to heaven. He said, "John truly baptized with water, but you shall be baptized with the Holy Spirit not many days from now" (Acts 1:5). When we become Christians, we're given a measure of the Holy Spirit. Every born-again believer has the Spirit of God within them. The more we surrender our lives to Christ, the more the Holy Spirit controls us. Christians are operating with varying degrees of the Spirit in them. Those who have received the baptism of the Holy Spirit are completely filled with the Spirit.

Who is the Holy Spirit?

The Holy Spirit is a Person. He is God just as is the Father and the Son. The Holy Spirit is the Spirit of God. The Bible tells us that Christ is now seated at the right hand of the Father in heaven. The only member of the Trinity on earth is the Spirit of God. The Holy Spirit is the power of God. Everything that God does on earth is done through the Person of the Holy Spirit.

If you ask an unbeliever about the Holy Spirit, he most likely couldn't tell you anything about Him. That's because He was not given to the world. The wonderful workings of the Spirit are not available to unbelievers. "The Spirit of truth, whom the world cannot receive, because it neither sees Him nor knows Him; but you know Him, for He dwells with you and will be in you" (John 14:17). Jesus gave the Holy Spirit to the Church, not to the world.

Everyone who has placed their faith in Christ is saved and has a measure of the Holy Spirit. It isn't necessary to have the baptism of the Holy Spirit in order to be saved. Many Christians are doing much work in God's kingdom with this gift.

Pastor Ron Phillips, of Central Baptist Church in Hixon, Tennessee, states in his book, *Awakened by the Spirit,*

> "Although the believer receives the Holy Spirit at conversion, He is *released* to work in the believer's life

at the baptism of the Holy Spirit. Many would say that the positional baptism of 1 Corinthians 12:13 is the same as the powerful baptism of Luke 3:16. But if it is the same, then where is the power of God on your people? Where is the evidence in their character and witness? Where is the unmistakable seal of God's fire and power? You see, it just doesn't add up."

(Page 14)[1]

1 Corinthians 12:13 states, "For by one Spirit we were all baptized into one body—whether Jews or Greeks, whether slaves or free—and have all been made to drink into one Spirit. Luke 3:16 states, "John answered, saying to all, 'I indeed baptize you with water; but One mightier than I is coming, whose sandal strap I am not worthy to loose. He will baptize you with the Holy Spirit and fire."

Let's consider this matter from God's point of view. He has given the Church power through the baptism of the Holy Spirit. Along with this power comes other gifts to build the church, but many believers don't take advantage of this gift. How God must be grieved as He sees this power not being used among some believers.

I believe His position would be like the following illustration: Let's say you built a house for your parents. It's designed specifically for their use. You spare no expense in its construction. It has the best of everything. You purchase expensive real-estate in the best section of town. It's beautifully landscaped, and the house is built with the finest quality possible. You present it to your parents. Then your aunts, uncles and cousins tell them that that house was not intended for them. "You can't live there," they say. "That house was not built for you!" Your heart is broken as your parents listen to their other relatives rather than you. The beautiful home you built sits empty as your mom and dad live in a house that is far less than what you intended for them.

This is how God must feel as some of the wonderful gifts of the Spirit go unused in most churches because people say, "It's not for us!"

At one time, Pastor Ron Phillips preached against the baptism of the Holy Spirit. Like many other Christians, he believed that tongues ended after the first century. He regarded those who spoke in tongues as not quite as spiritual as himself. Then he received the baptism of the Holy Spirit. Now, all the gifts of the Spirit are used in his church. He's a Southern Baptist, and Southern Baptists don't speak in tongues. His book tells about his journey of receiving the baptism of the Holy Spirit and how the Spirit has transformed Central Baptist Church.

There are two ways of receiving the baptism of the Holy Spirit. The most common is by the laying on of hands. Someone who is Spirit-filled lays hands on the head of the candidate and prays for him. Some people receive this gift on their own by just asking for it.

Pastor Phillips explains in his book how to receive the baptism of the Holy Spirit (Page 17).

> Be sure you are saved.
>
> Confess your sins.
>
> Surrender to Jesus afresh, and give Him the right to do whatever He wants in your life.
>
> Tell Him you want everything He has for you.

Ask Him for the baptism (filling, sealing) with the Holy Spirit.

Allow Him to take control of your spirit-man—the inner you.

Respond to His move as He leads and endows.

Praise Him as He leads in His fullness and power. [2]

When a person has received the baptism of the Holy Spirit, the fruit of the Spirit is more evident in their life. "The fruit of the Spirit is love, joy, peace, longsuffering, kindness, goodness, faithfulness, gentleness, self control" (Galatians 5:22–23). This fruit is for every child of God, not just for those who have the full-measure of the Holy Spirit. The more people surrender their lives to Christ, the more the fruit of the Spirit is evident. We are to continually be filled with the Spirit; and as that happens, the fruit of the Spirit becomes manifested.

The difference between the gifts of the Spirit and the fruit of the Spirit is that the fruit produces character and the gifts of the Spirit are tools to build the church. Every Christian is given at least one spiritual gift, regardless of whether they have received the baptism of the Holy Spirit or not. There are some gifts that are only available to believers after they are full of the Spirit. These are discussed in the next chapter.

When we receive the baptism of the Holy Spirit, we're completely filled with the Spirit, and speak in tongues. "They were all filled with the Holy Spirit and began to speak with other tongues, as the Spirit gave them utterance" (Acts 2:4).

When I received the baptism of the Holy Spirit several years ago, I only spoke a few syllables in tongues. That's all I can do today. I've asked God on many occasions to give me more of a prayer language, but so far, it hasn't happened. I use prayer language because that's what speaking in tongues is when it is done for personal use. (This is not to be confused with the gift of tongues which is used in the church.) The Spirit prays on our behalf, and we are edified, or built up. "He who speaks in a tongue edifies himself" (1 Corinthians 14:4).

I like Oral Roberts's explanation of how the Holy Spirit prays for us in his book, *The Baptism of the Holy Spirit*.

> "I am told that, among other things, a psychiatrist is a professionally trained listener who knows how to question you so that you can talk about the things hidden and repressed in your spirit that are troubling you. The psychiatrist searches and finds ways to help you bring them out into the open and talk them out. Then you feel released. The Holy Spirit is a divine Therapist. He gets down inside your inner being and finds these things that are troubling you. As you speak in the language of the Spirit, the therapy is going on and that is why you feel instantly relieved or edified.
>
> "This does not mean that speaking in tongues is a 'cure-all.' It does mean that God responds and places divine aids at your disposal."[3]

Even though I can't speak in tongues fluently, I do know that I received the baptism of the Holy Spirit because of the positive changes that have taken place in my life. I'm convicted of sin much sooner now. Before this experience, my Christian life was characterized by ups and downs. Sometimes, I was close to God, and at other times I struggled in my faith. When I received the full measure of the Holy Spirit, my life became more consistent. I live a holier life now. The Holy Spirit is there to convict me of sin in an instant.

Another change is that I truly worship God. Since I have been worshiping God in spirit and in truth, I have found supernatural favor with the Lord. He seems to pour out His blessings on me. When we combine worship along with holy living, we put ourselves in a position to receive all God has for us.

After I received the baptism of the Holy Spirit and saw how much it changed my life, I wondered why I didn't receive it sooner. Then I thought of how much I have benefited from being a Southern Baptist all my adult life. Southern Baptists are known as "people of the Word."

Teaching the Bible is an important part of their program. Also, they stress soul winning. I'm thankful for the knowledge of the Bible I received and the ability to lead others to Christ. I can see the hand of God directing my life in a way that fulfills God's plan for me. God is directing each level of my growth. God does that for each of us; He directs our path when we commit our life to Him.

I had quite an amazing experience the week I receive the baptism of the Holy Spirit. It seemed that the love of God came upon me in a way that I can't describe. It was such an intimate experience with God that I haven't told many people about it. I don't know how to put into words exactly what I felt, but I experienced a tremendous love, joy and power from God.

I also received a tremendous power to witness for the Lord which only lasted a few days. During that time, I took an elderly lady to the emergency room at a near by hospital. While I was there, I had a conversation with a young black man who had been injured in an attempted robbery. He was perhaps in his early twenties. He had come into the hospital accompanied by two police officers. One officer talked to him about getting his life together. I knew the officer probably wouldn't have success because he wasn't getting to the root of this man's problem—a sinful heart. You have to change someone's sin problem before you can successfully deal with other areas of their life.

I waited for the officer to finish speaking. Then I spoke to this man boldly, under the direction of the Holy Spirit. I said, "Do you wish you could have a fresh start in your life, with no past sins?"

"Ya, that would be nice," he said. He didn't show much interest until my next statement.

"Jesus Christ can come into your heart and take away all your past sins and make you completely clean. Your sins can be forgiven, just as if they never happened. You'll still have to face the consequences of your actions, but you can have a new life in Christ."

He looked as if he was pondering my words. I went on to speak to him with the same boldness and power that Peter had on the Day of Pentecost. Somehow, the

Spirit of God worked through me to reach his spirit. The Spirit knew what to say to him and he listened intently.

I glanced at the two officers in the corner. They looked at me in amazement. Perhaps they were wondering how I was able to speak so powerfully. Frankly, I was astonished at what I was saying. I had never spoken that boldly and forcefully before. It was the power of the Holy Spirit in me. I couldn't do that on my own. In a few minutes that man bowed his head and asked Christ into his heart.

I went to the waiting room later, where I struck up a conversation with a man about the same age as the first. This one was not escorted by police officers, but he had a different bondage, though. As I talked to him, he told me he was living with a woman he was not married to. The Holy Spirit began His work once again. In a gentle, but convicting tone, the Holy Spirit spoke through me. I couldn't believe the words that came out of my mouth. They certainly were not my own.

In a few moments, he confessed his sins and made a commitment to live for the Lord. He told me he had already given his heart to the Lord, but he wasn't living for Him.

Now, I don't normally speak to strangers this way, especially to men. What happened that day was the Holy Spirit working through me. That is the power that is released through the baptism of the Holy Spirit. The Holy Spirit chose to give me that gift for only a few days. I wonder what I would have done if it had remained with me. Now, I still tell people about Jesus many places I go, but I don't have that same power as I did that week.

We have no control over the Holy Spirit. He works in our lives as He chooses. Jesus made reference to this when He said, "The wind blows where it wishes, and you hear the sound of it, but cannot tell where it comes from and where it is going" (John 3:8).

What happened to me is an example of how the Holy Spirit gives the gifts of the Spirit. An example of this is with D. L. Moody, the great evangelist. Early in his ministry, two ladies told him he needed the baptism of the Holy Spirit to give him more power in preaching. This annoyed him because he thought he was already a good preacher. They told him he was working in his own strength. He was not pleased with these ladies and dismissed what they said.

They did not dismiss him, though. They secretly prayed for him every day. Soon he began to ponder what they had said. Could it be true? Was he really preaching in his own strength? Eventually, he did receive the baptism of the Holy Spirit.

Someone once said to Moody, "The world has yet to see what God will do through a man fully consecrated to Him." Moody was determined to be such a man. Through his ministry, thousands came to know the Lord. He had the power of the baptism of the Holy Spirit along with the gift of evangelism, and a total commitment to Christ. Actually, it wasn't D. L. Moody who was so powerful. It was a powerful God who worked through him. His influence is still felt throughout the world today, even though he died at the end of the nineteenth century.

What could God accomplish through you with a full-measure of the Holy Spirit and a life totally dedicated to Him? God has a plan for your life, and He will give you power to do it if you allow Him. The Holy Spirit will also give you the tools you'll need to get your assignment done. In the next chapter, we'll take a look at the nine gifts of the Spirit, or tools, that Paul mentions in 1 Corinthians 12.

Endnotes

1. Ron Phillips. *Awakened by the Spirit* (Nashville, TN: Thomas Nelson Publishers, 1999), p14
2. Ibid, 17
3. Oral Roberts, *The Baptism of the Holy Spirit* (Tulsa, Ok: Oral Roberts, 1975) p. 49.

TOOLS FOR THE BUILDERS

One afternoon, a pastor and his wife were visiting in the home of a young woman. During the visit, the Holy Spirit spoke a word of knowledge to the pastor's wife that the woman was planning to leave her husband. The pastor's wife said nothing at that time, but the next day, she visited the woman by herself. She told her what the Lord had revealed to her. The woman acknowledged that this was true. The pastor's wife counseled her at that time; and as a result, her marriage was saved.

This is an example of how a word of knowledge is intended to be used in the church. It's one of the nine manifestation gifts mentioned in 1 Corinthians 12:8–10. These gifts provide a dimension to the Christian life that some believers don't know exist. Paul tells us, "Concerning spiritual gifts, brethren, I do not want you to be ignorant" (1 Corinthians 12:1). If you're one of those who are uninformed, this chapter will help you understand the nine manifestation gifts.

Paul says, "But the manifestation of the Spirit is given to each one for the profit of all: for to one is given the word of wisdom through the Spirit, to another

> the word of knowledge through the same Spirit, to another faith by the same Spirit, to another gifts of healing by the same Spirit, to another the working of miracles, to another prophecy, to another discerning of spirits, to another different kinds of tongues, to another the interpretation of tongues. But one and the same Spirit works all these things, distributing to each one individually as He wills."
>
> 1 Corinthians 12:7–11

As we saw in the last chapter, these nine spiritual gifts are given by the Holy Spirit to those He chooses; but they're only available to those who have received the baptism of the Holy Spirit.

But why are these gifts only available to those who are completely filled with the Spirit?

The manifestation gifts differ from other spiritual gifts in that they deal in the supernatural. By the time you finish reading this chapter, you'll have a clear understanding of why these gifts aren't given automatically when we place our trust in Jesus. These supernatural gifts are "power tools" used to build the church. Not every believer needs these because not everyone is a builder in God's kingdom. "Sunday morning Christians" do little or no work in the church. Others are carnal Christians who live as the natural man does. These believers don't need power tools. Giving these gifts to them would be comparable to giving an electric drill to a five year-old. These nine gifts are for serious builders in God's kingdom. That's the reason they're not automatically given at salvation.

In the previous chapter, we saw how believers are baptized in the Holy Spirit. Generally, Christians ask for and receive this gift by the laying on of hands, and then speak in tongues; but some have received this gift without asking. Speaking in tongues is a sign or a token. Jesus said, "These signs will follow those who believe: In My name they will cast out demons; they will speak with new tongues" (Mark 16:17). With the baptism of the Holy Spirit, believers receive power, boldness, and a greater degree of holiness.

In time, other manifestation gifts begin to operate in their life. The Holy Spirit chooses which gifts to give. To one person, He gives the gift of prophecy, and to another He gives the gifts of healing and miracles. God equips each of us with the manifestation gifts we need to accomplish the task He has given us. Paul tells us, "One and the same Spirit works all these things, distributing to each one individually as He wills" (1 Corinthians 12:11).

Millions of believers around the world are using these gifts just as the church in Jerusalem did. What is recorded in the book of Acts is an example for us. Congregations who have all these function more efficiently because they're using all their tools. Can churches operate successfully without them? Yes, they can—and many are; but Christians could do even more if they had all their tools.

Consider that for thousands of years, people lived without electricity, computers, and air planes. Think how much these modern inventions have enriched our lives. In the same way, the church has generally been without the manifestation gifts for centuries; and it has functioned adequately without them. In the last hundred years or so, these gifts have been reintroduced to the church; and they're now in operation as they were in the book of Acts. Just as the above modern inventions dramatically enhanced our lives, the manifestation gifts have enriched the church, and these gifts are rapidly restoring the body of Christ to the way it originally operated at the time of the apostles.

Why was the church without these gifts for the past two thousand years? Well, actually, it hasn't been. The baptism of the Holy Spirit never completely left the church. Throughout the centuries, some have been filled with the Spirit. Men like Charles and John Wesley, the founders of the Methodist Church, were spirit-filled and spoke in tongues. All who possessed this gift were looked upon with suspicion and often persecuted; causing them to go underground.

Then in the beginning of the twentieth century, the baptism of the Holy Spirit was reintroduced to the church. The early pioneers of the charismatic movement were viewed with mistrust and often persecuted. The persecution has stopped, but some still look upon spirit-filled believers with misgivings.

I believe one reason God has brought the baptism of the Holy Spirit back to the church in these final days is to bring lost souls into the kingdom. Those who are spirit-filled possess power and boldness to witness to the lost. In the previous chapter, I related how I became a bold witness for the Lord after I received the baptism of the Holy Spirit. This is happening to many Christians around the word, and as a result; millions are professing faith in Christ.

Now let's see how each of the nine manifestation gifts operates.

The Gift of the Word of Wisdom

The first is the word of wisdom. This gift concerns God's revelation of His secrets and plans. Since He is revealing only a small part of what He knows, this gift is called a word of wisdom rather than the gift of wisdom. All the secrets of the universe are known to God. The word of wisdom deals with the secret plans that He chooses to unveil. The purpose of revealing these is always to further His kingdom.

Paul gives an example of a word of wisdom that was revealed after Jesus was crucified: "We speak the wisdom of God in a mystery, the hidden wisdom which God ordained before the ages for our glory, which none of the rulers of this age knew; for had they known, they would not have crucified the Lord of glory" (1 Corinthians 2:7–8). In the above verses, we find God kept the plan of salvation hidden in order that Jesus could die for the sins of the world.

God has secrets of the universe that He will share with those who have the baptism of the Holy Spirit and an intimate relationship with Him. How does He communicate these? The Holy Spirit speaks a word of wisdom into the mind of a person He chooses. Whatever He chooses to reveal will benefit the church in some way.

I belong to Watchman's Brigade, an intercessory prayer group that meets once a month to pray for Israel. On different occasions, the Holy Spirit has given us a word of wisdom. The messages have always revealed some of God's plans concerning Israel and America. This gave us a better understanding of what is happening and we became better intercessors for Israel.

Sometimes, a word of wisdom concerns judgment. God reveals His plans to judge nations today, just as He did in the Old Testament. Amos tells us, "Surely the Lord God does nothing, unless He reveals His secret to His servants the prophets" (Amos 3:7). This gift is not limited to judgment. It concerns any plans or secrets that God chooses to reveal.

The Gift of the Word of Knowledge

The gift of the word of knowledge is similar to the word of wisdom. Instead of revealing God's plans, thought this gift reveals facts concerning the past or the present.

An example of a word of knowledge occurs in the book of Acts. Ananias and Sapphira sold some land and lied about the price they received. "Peter said, 'Ananias, why has Satan filled your heart to lie to the Holy Spirit and keep back part of the price of the land for yourself?'" (Acts 5:3). The Holy Spirit gave Peter a word of knowledge concerning Ananias and Sapphira's sin.

An example of a modern-day word of knowledge occurs daily on the 700 *Club*. Pat Robertson, or another host of the program, gives a word of knowledge concerning someone watching at home whom God is healing.

Faith

At times, the work in God's kingdom seems to be impossible. In the natural, it couldn't happen. That's when the supernatural gift of faith is needed. These go beyond the faith we all have to be saved. It's the kind of faith that trusts God for miracles. It's the kind of faith that moves mountains.

When Paul Crouch attempted to broadcast his first television station, the signal wouldn't go over the mountain. He had spent all his money on the station, but it seemed that his efforts were in vain because the signal was blocked. He spoke to the mountain just as Jesus commanded. He spoke and believed that the signal would go over the mountain—and it did. His supernatural faith believed God for a miracle.

The book of Acts tells about Barnabas, who had the gift of faith. "He was a good man, full of the Holy Spirit and of faith. And a great many people were added to the Lord" (Acts 11:24). Stephen also had this gift. "Stephen, full of faith and power, did great wonders and signs among the people" (Acts 6:8). Did you notice that not only did these men have an abundance of faith; they both were full of the Holy Spirit? They both did mighty works as a result. The New Testament mentions many believers, but not all of them were said to be full of faith.

The Holy Spirit gives an extra measure of faith to believers when we need it. This faith is given for the purpose of fulfilling a particular task in the kingdom of God. The Holy Spirit equips us with the tools we need to fulfill whatever God has given us to do. Sometimes, we receive a word of wisdom or a word of knowledge. Other times, we receive an extra measure of faith.

The Gifts of Healings

All Christians should pray for the sick, and many times people are healed as a result of our prayers; but this isn't the same as the supernatural gifts of healing. The Holy

Spirit gives this gift to some individuals who enable them to lay hands on the sick and many times they are healed. Notice that it is the gifts of healing.

An example of someone with this gift is Kenneth Hagin. In his book, *The Holy Spirit and His Gifts,* he explains that he believes these are gifts of healing because there are many types of diseases. Hagin mentioned that he has success in healing some types of illnesses, but not others. Other people get different illnesses healed.[3] Of course, it's the Holy Spirit, not Kenneth Hagin, who actually does the healing. The Spirit also decides who will receive this supernatural gift.

The Working of Miracles

While Jesus was on earth, He preformed many miracles. He fed 5,000 people with five small loafs and two fishes. He also raised the dead. When Jesus returned to heaven, His followers were filled with the Spirit and continued to work wonders. Those filled with the Spirit today sometime experience miracles just as the apostles did.

An example of a miracle occurred with a missionary overseas. She and her husband ran an orphanage with 120 children. One day, they had no food. A woman from the American embassy came with a pot of chili and some rice. The woman brought only enough for the missionary's family of four. She didn't realize that they had 120 children to be fed. The missionary wondered what to do. Then a voice spoke to her, "Trust Me. I will provide. Give the children the chili and rice." Immediately, she dipped the chili into the children's bowls. There was enough for all of them and her family!

How comforting it is to know that these supernatural events are not just for Bible times. God is able and willing to perform miracles today just as He did then.

The Gift of Prophecy

Several years ago, I taught weight-lose and nutrition classes in several churches; but I felt a strong desire to write full-time. I wondered if the Lord was leading me in this direction. Then one day in a restaurant, a woman I had never met said to me, "I have a word from the Lord for you. You will be the author of many books." God used her to confirm what I felt in my heart was the direction He was leading me. I'm thankful for that confirmation.

The above is an example of the gift of prophecy. Paul tells us we're to desire spiritual gifts, especially the gift of prophecy. What makes this one so special? I believe it's because this one offers the greatest benefit to the church. This gives direction, encouragement, or admonishment to a believer. We all need guidance at sometimes in our lives. God provides it through this gift. This isn't the only way God speaks to us today. Sometimes He speaks through other people, in our minds, in our dreams, and through pastors and teachers. Of course, His main method is still to speak through His Written Word. Whatever method He uses, He will never contradict the Bible.

The gift of prophecy is God's avenue of communicating with Christians in specific situations just as the Bible is God's way of communicating with all people of all times. When a Christian is discouraged, a message from God spoken through the gift of prophecy can bring encouragement. When someone is going down the wrong path, the Spirit can warn him to forsake his sin and return to God. When someone is uncertain about what to do, the Spirit advises them. Who among us has not needed a word from God from time to time?

The misuse of personal prophecy has caused a mistrust of this gift. Sometimes, a person will claim to have a message from God that isn't actually from the Lord. As a result, some have given up their jobs, their homes, and made numerous other bad decisions. A prophecy should confirm what you already believe, and the message should never contradict the Bible. When I received the prophecy concerning my life, it confirmed what I already felt in my heart.

One example of the misuse of prophecy is found in the book, *Surprised by the Power of the Spirit,* by Jack Deere. He tells of a man and woman who had been dating and then broke up when the man realized this woman was not the one he wanted to marry. Someone gave him a message that it was God's will that they get married. They didn't love each other, and didn't want to spend their lives together; but neither wanted to disobey God. Because they failed to confirm that the prophecy was from God, they got married, and their marriage was a disaster and ended in divorce. If only they have sought the Lord on this matter! [2]

The gift of prophecy extends beyond personal prophecy—it's also used in the church. In this setting, it functions the same way as tongues and interruption of tongues. The message is given to the entire congregation. Paul explains that prophecy is better than speaking in tongues if visitors are present:

> "If the whole church comes together in one place, and all speak with tongues, and there come in those who are uninformed or unbelievers, will they not say that you are out of your mind? But if all prophesy, and an unbeliever or an uninformed person comes in, he is convinced by all, he is convicted by all. And thus the secrets of his heart are revealed; and so, falling down on his face, he will worship God and report that God is truly among you."
>
> 1 Corinthians 14:23–25

One morning, the following prophecy was given at Evangel Temple: "If you have a drug addiction, come to Me, and I will free you." Immediately after this was given, two young men across the aisle from me left the church in a hurry. In fact, they nearly ran out of the sanctuary. As Paul said, the secrets of your heart will be laid bare.

The Discerning of Spirits

The person who has the gift of discerning of spirits can tell when someone is operating under the influence of the Holy Spirit or an evil spirit. For example, sometimes a preacher or Bible teacher will proclaim a message that is not compatible with the Scripture. Perhaps he claims to have some special revelation or truth that no one else has. He might sound convincing and even quote the Bible, but his message is from the father of lies—the old devil himself. Those who have the gift of discerning of spirits can tell when someone is operating under the influence of demonic spirits.

Different Kinds of Tongues and Interpretation of Tongues

The gift of tongues is God's way of communicating with the church, just as is prophecy; but many Christians fight vigorously to keep this superb gift out of their congregation. How much they are missing! These uninformed believers are keeping the door closed to an important avenue God uses to speak to the church. If they would diligently search the Scriptures and seek God's face, rather than believe what others say, they would reap the benefits of this gift as well as all the other manifestation gifts.

This gift is called different kinds of tongues because there are many languages that can be used. The person is speaking in a language that they have never learned but is spoken somewhere in the world. The second chapter of Acts records that visitors to Jerusalem heard the gospel preached in their native tongue, and as a result, many were added to the church that day. I read of two examples of people who came to Christ by hearing a message in tongues while they were visiting in another country, just as happened on the day of Pentecost.

Both the gift of tongues and prophecy are intended to comfort, warn, and advise. When they are used in the church, these gifts are interchangeable. Paul said,

> "I wish you all spoke with tongues, but even more that you prophesied; for he who prophesies is greater than he who speaks with tongues, unless indeed he interprets, that the church may receive edification."
> 1 Corinthians 14:5

Through the gifts of tongues and interpretations of tongues, God speaks directly to people's need, just as with the gift of prophecy. When the church meets, the Holy Spirit gives a message for that particular congregation. The Holy Spirit directs someone to use the gift of tongues. That person is unaware of what he is saying. After the message is given, someone else gives the interpretation. Paul tells us that we are to weigh carefully what is said. When the King of the universe chooses to warn, comfort and advise us, we should pay attention.

At Evangel Temple, the messages given through tongues and interpretation of tongues often concern healing, witnessing to the lost, or trusting God in difficult situations; but the messages can concern anything. It's thrilling to know that the God of the universe is speaking directly to our congregation.

The gift of different kinds of tongues is not the same as speaking in tongues. Everyone who has received the baptism of the Holy Spirit speaks in tongues, but not everyone is given the gift of tongues. The gift of tongues is only given to a few individuals and is used in the church. The Holy Spirit prompts him to give a message. Every person who has the baptism of the Holy Spirit speaks in tongues. Jesus said, "These signs will follow those who believe: In My name they will cast out demons; they will speak with new tongues" (Mark 16:17). The purpose of speaking in tongues is to edify, or build up the believer. Sometimes, it's referred to as a prayer language, where one prays in tongues. The gift of speaking in tongues is used in a worship service; it comforts, advises, and warns believers.

Conclusion

After reading this chapter, you can see why these manifestation gifts are only given to those who have the baptism of the Holy Spirit. Can you imagine a "Sunday morning Christian" having the gift of miracles or the gifts of healing? What a waste that would be. That's the reason we usually have to ask for the baptism of the Holy Spirit. Then the Holy Spirit gives us the gifts He wants us to have. These power tools are to be used by serious builders in God's kingdom.

If you had to eliminate one of these gifts from the church, which one would you choose? That would be difficult because each one is distinct and important. Yet many Christians are doing God's work without any of these.

Millions of Christians around the world are baptized with the Holy Spirit and have access to the nine manifestation gifts. In some countries, the majority of Christians are completely filled with the Spirit. God is able to accomplish much in churches that are using all the tools available to them.

Endnotes

1. Jack Deere, *Surprised by the Power of the Spirit* (Grand Rapids: Zondervan, 1993).
2. Kenneth E. Hagin, *The Holy Spirit and His Gifts* (Tulsa, Ok: Kenneth Hagin Ministries, Inc., 1982) page 97.

Spiritual Warfare—How to Battle the Devil and Win

Who dominates the earth? Is it God? Man? Satan? As we saw in an earlier chapter, it's Satan. In the Scriptures, he's referred to as the god of this world and the prince of the power of the air. His power is limited though; God keeps him on a leash, but how did he gain any control at all?

It started in the Garden of Eden. After God created Adam, He gave him dominion over the earth. Adam was to rule as God's representative. God had, and continues to have, ultimate authority, but Adam was His manager. Adam's position could be compared to the Secretary of State.

How wonderful was Adam and Eve's existence in the Garden of Eden! God actually walked and talked with them. They lived in perfect tranquility with no sickness, distress or death. But God gave them a stern warning: "The Lord God commanded the man, saying, 'Of every tree of the garden you may freely eat; but of the tree of the knowledge of good and evil you shall not eat, for in the day that you eat of it you shall surely die" (Genesis 2:16–17).

Death in this verse means spiritual death, which is separation from God. On the day they would eat from the forbidden tree, God would no longer walk and talk with Adam and Eve in the Garden of Eden. Later, they would die physically.

Adam and Eve lived in perfect tranquility until the devil deceived Eve by telling her, "You will not surely die. For God knows that in the day you eat of it your eyes will be opened, and you will be like God, knowing good and evil" (Genesis 3:4–5).

Adam and Eve both ate from the tree of the knowledge of good and evil. As a result of Adam's sin, he lost dominion of the earth; and Satan now has dominance. Evil entered the earth, along with universal sinfulness, suffering, corruption, decay and physical death. Satan became the ruler of this world system, although God is still sovereign over all of creation.

Just because he's referred to as the god of this world doesn't mean he is all-powerful. No one in the universe, not even Satan, has the authority and power that God has. "The Lord Himself is God in heaven above and on the earth beneath; there is no other" (Deuteronomy 4:39). That means no one is God's equal. Satan is a created being, and he will always be under God's control. The devil might have power over this world system, but God has ultimate authority.

But where did the devil and evil come from? Wasn't everything God created good?

We can see from the first chapter of Genesis that all God created was good. There was no evil anywhere in creation, neither in heaven nor on earth. Paul informs us in Colossians that Jesus created all things. "By Him all things were created that are in heaven and that are on earth, visible and invisible, whether thrones or dominions or principalities or powers. All things were created through Him and for Him" (Colossians 1:16). Thrones, dominions, principalities, and powers refer to various ranks of spirit beings. And everything that was created in both worlds was good. Now let's find out were evil came from.

Lucifer, the son of the morning

Indeed, everything God created was good. That included Lucifer, who later became Satan. He was at one time an archangel, the highest ranking of angels. The Bible mentions only three archangels: Lucifer, Michael, and Gabriel. The book of Ezekiel describes Lucifer:

> "You were the seal of perfection, full of wisdom and perfect in beauty. You were in Eden, the garden of God. Every precious stone was your covering: the sardius, topaz, and diamond, beryl, onyx, and jasper, sapphire, turquoise, and emerald with gold. The workmanship of your timbrels and pipes was prepared for you on the day you were created...You were perfect in your ways from the day you were created till iniquity was found in you"
> Ezekiel 28:12–13, 15

How beautiful Lucifer must have been! He was covered with sparkling precious stones. And how beautiful was his sound! He was created with musical instruments to praise and worship God. In his book, *Your Adversary the Devil*, J.

Dwight Pentecost says of Lucifer's music: "Lucifer didn't have to look for someone to play the organ so that he could sing the doxology—he was the doxology. The very beauty of God reflected through Lucifer brought praises and honor and glory to God."

But Lucifer wasn't satisfied to worship God; he desired to *be* god and take God's place on His throne. He said, "I will ascend into heaven. I will exalt my throne above the stars of God....I will be like the Most High" (Isaiah 14:13–14). That's when Lucifer was cast out of heaven, and one third of the angels followed him.

Because we can't see them, some believe that the devil and demons aren't real, but they are! They're invisible spirit beings and they're just as real as what we see in the natural world. "We do not wrestle against flesh and blood, but against principalities, against powers, against the rulers of darkness of this age, against spiritual hosts of wickedness in the heavenly places" (Ephesians 6:12). They tempt us, deceive us and try every way possible to get us to rebel against God as they have.

Come with me as we observe Satan in operation. We see the accuser approach the throne of God with a bit of gossip about some human being. "Did you see that?" Satan jeers. "There's another man stealing and lying again. Those people You created are constantly breaking Your commandments." The devil goes on to tell about other sins he has observed that day, for it's true that there's none righteous on the earth. God is aware of every sin that mankind commits. And the devil delights in pointing out mankind's transgressions. Day after day, God listened to the accusations that the devil brought against those He created in His image, the one's He loves so dearly.

Then one day, God did something about man's sin problem. He put into place the plan He had from the foundation of the world. God sent His beloved Son, His only begotten Son, to earth. And on a dark day in Jerusalem, that precious One was nailed to a cross. All the sins that you and I have committed were nailed to that cross also.

The last words Jesus uttered on the cross were, "It is finished" (John 19:30). The word finished is *tetelestai*, meaning paid in full. Jesus paid in full the sin debt we owe. The indictment of sin against us has been paid. That's what Paul meant when he wrote,

> "Having wiped out the handwriting of requirements that was against us, which was contrary to us. And He has taken it out of the way, having nailed it to the cross. Having disarmed principalities and powers, He made a public spectacle of them, triumphing over them in it."
>
> Colossians 2:14–15

Satan and his demons were defeated at the cross. The accuser can no longer bring any charge of sin against the child of God. "There is therefore now no condemnation to those who are in Christ Jesus" (Romans 8:1). The devil has no power over us unless we give it to him for Christ defeated the devil with His precious blood. "For this purpose the Son of God was manifested, that He might destroy the works of the devil" (1 John 3:8).

Our Authority over Satan

Paul also tells us,

> "He (God) raised Him from the dead and seated Him at His right hand in the heavenly places, far above all principality and power and might and dominion, and every name that is named, not only in this age but also in that which is to come. And he put all things under His feet, and gave Him to be head over all things to the church....And you He made alive, who were dead in trespasses and sins,...and raised us up together, and made us sit together in the heavenly places in Christ Jesus."
>
> Ephesians 1:20–22, 2:1,6

Wow! This verse tells us that we also have authority over demonic spirits just as Christ has. Even though these spirits are created higher than we are, we have authority over them because we're joined with Christ; and we now have *His* authority.

Even though Jesus defeated the devil at the cross, it is our responsibility to enforce the conquest. Satan will not be totally conquered until Christ returns at the end of this age. That means the devil is still allowed to attack us even though he's been defeated. God has a purpose for allowing Satan to continue to work on earth, as we'll see later in this chapter. While we await Satan's final defeat, we have to enforce the conquest that Jesus won. And we can because we have been joined with Christ. Every Christian has authority over demonic spirits just as Jesus has.

Because you're a child of God and have authority over Satan and his demons, they are your enemy. They're out to destroy you. The devil already has the natural man in his possession. It's the spiritual man he's after. Satan and his demons will try to keep you from accomplishing God's plan for your life; they'll try to destroy your reputation, and even kill you if possible. They attempt to accomplish these by placing temptations in your mind. That's how demonic spirits work. They have access to your mind and whisper into your conscious. As bad as they are, they're not our only source of temptation. They're just one member of the unholy trinity.

The Unholy Trinity

It's not only demonic spirits that tempt us. We face temptation from all three members of the unholy trinity—the flesh, the world, and Satan. We've seen so far in this chapter how Satan operates; now let's take a look at the flesh and the world. We need to be aware of these for to be forewarned is to be forearmed.

Let's consider the flesh, that part of our human nature that is prone to sin. Every human being battles the flesh. In fact, the majority of our temptations come from our flesh. It's true that we face satanic attacks at times, but we battle the flesh every day.

Paul tells us, "The works of the flesh are evident, which are: adultery, fornication, uncleanness, lewdness, idolatry, sorcery, hatred, contentions, jealousies, outburst of wrath, selfish ambitions, dissensions, heresies, envy, murders, drunkenness, revelries, and the like; (Galatians 5:19–21).

We find ourselves at war between what we know is right and what our flesh urges us to do. "The flesh lusts against the Spirit, and the Spirit against the flesh; and these are contrary to one another, so that you do not do the things that you wish" (Galatians 5:17). Can't you identify with that? I know I can. Thankfully, there's hope for us. "Walk in the Spirit, and you shall not fulfill the lust of the flesh" (Galatians 5:16). When we're controlled by the Holy Spirit, we'll want to please God more that to satisfy our flesh. It's important to keep our thoughts pleasing to God. "Those who live according to the flesh set their minds on the things of the flesh, but those who live according to the Spirit, the things of the Spirit. For to be carnally minded is death, but to be spiritually minded is life and peace" (Romans 8:5–6).

We need to bring every thought into captivity. Paul tells us

> "Whatever things are true, whatever things are noble, whatever things are just, whatever things are pure, whatever things are lovely, whatever things are of good report, if there is any virtue and if there is anything praiseworthy—meditate on these things."
>
> Philippians 4:8

We also face temptations of the world. The world tempts us with money, power, and recognition. John tells us,

> "Do not love the world or the things in the world. If anyone loves the world, the love of the Father is not in him. For all that is in the world—the lust of the flesh, the lust of the eyes, and the pride of life—is not

of the Father but is of the world. And the world is passing away, and the lust of it; but he who does the will of God abides forever."

1 John 2:15–17

Every born-again child of God can have victory over temptations from all members of the unholy trinity. James tells us, "Submit to God. Resist the devil and he will flee from you. Draw near to God and He will draw near to you" (James 4:7–8). These two verses are powerful; every Christian should commit them to memory.

We're in a life-long battle with temptation. Let's now examine the weapons God has given us to fight this conflict. This isn't a traditional war as the ones we fight in the natural world. Paul tells us "We do not wrestle against flesh and blood, but against principalities, against powers, against the rulers of the darkness of this age, against spiritual hosts of wickedness in the heavenly places" (Ephesians 6:12).

Because we're not in a conventional war, the weapons we use aren't conventional either. "Though we walk in the flesh, we do not war according to the flesh, for the weapons of our warfare are not carnal but mighty in God for pulling down of strongholds" (2 Corinthians 10:3–4). Let's take a look at this mighty arsenal.

You can read about God's battle plan in Ephesians, chapter six. In this chapter, Paul uses the analogy of the armor of a Roman soldier. The Roman soldier was well-equipped for combat; his armor protected him from head to foot. You, too, can be well protected from assaults from Satan. Paul tells us to put on the whole armor so that we can stand in the evil day. The evil day refers to any day you come under attack. This armor will be effective against all of the unholy trinity—Satan, the flesh, and the world, but it's only effective if you wear the entire armor every day.

The armor begins with the belt of the truth. Where can you find truth? You won't find it in what the devil tells you. You won't find truth in this world system either. It's only found in the Word of God, and in Jesus Christ who said, "I am the way, the truth, and the life" (John 14:6). The words of Christ found in the Scripture are absolute, eternal truth, as is every word of the Bible. Paul tells us to put on the belt of truth. Before we can put on the truth, we must first know the truth, and that comes only by studying God's Word.

There's no validity in the devil, for "He was a murderer from the beginning, and does not stand in the truth, because there is no truth in him. When he speaks a lie, he speaks from his own resources, for he is a liar, and the father of it" (John 8:44).

In the world, Satan uses people as instruments to promote his lies. An example of this occurred on a television talk show a few years ago. A woman was encouraging teens and young adults to explore their sexuality. She explained how this was such a wonderful experience that young people shouldn't deny themselves, and she was encouraging them to have as many sexual encounters as they could.

As I listened to the lies she promoted, I wondered how many people were influenced by what she said. She didn't tell the truth about sexual sin. She didn't mention sexually transmitted diseases, unwanted pregnancies, abortions, loss of respect, or self-esteem. She didn't tell about babies born with AIDS or children wondering who their daddies are. Nor did she mention the plight of millions of children growing up in poverty without the discipline and financial support of a father in the home. She didn't talk about how this led to crime and a financial drain on society. No, she never once spoke the truth about having sex outside of marriage. Millions of people around the world heard her lies, and no doubt many believed them.

How can you protect yourselves from lies from the unholy trinity? Put on the belt of truth each day. Study God's Word and know the truth. Memorize Scripture. Then when the enemy tempts you with lies, you'll be armed with verses to refute them. "Your word I have hidden in my heart, that I might not sin against You" (Psalm 119:11).

If you have on the belt of truth, you'll know what the Bible says about every temptation you face. Somewhere in the Scripture there's a principle that will guide you. Here's more good news: "No temptation has overtaken you except such as is common to man; but God is faithful, who will not allow you to be tempted beyond what you are able, but with the temptation will also make the way of escape, that you may be able to bear it" (1 Corinthians 10:13). God has control over every temptation you face. He'll never allow you to be tempted beyond what you can bear.

Next is the breastplate of righteousness. Righteousness means having a right standing with God. A righteous person not only knows God's Word, but is committed to being a doer of the Word. He applies the truth that he knows from the Bible.

Does that mean he'll never sin again? No, none of us will ever be sinless in this life as Jesus was, but that's what we should strive for. Whenever a righteous person sins, they confess it quickly. They're filled with the Spirit and able to do as Paul says in Galatians, "Walk in the Spirit, and you shall not fulfill the lust of the flesh" (Galatians 5:16). A righteous person takes a firm stand against the attacks of the devil.

Your feet should be shod with the preparation of the gospel. That means be prepared ahead of time for attacks from Satan. It's too late to prepare once you're faced with temptation. The best preparation is to have an intimate relationship with Christ, spend time with Him each day and memorize Scripture. Many Christians have fallen into sin because they weren't properly prepared when temptation came.

Paul tells us there's two sins we're to flee—lust and idolatry. He says, "Flee also youthful lusts; but pursue righteousness, faith, love, peace with those who call on the Lord out of a pure heart" (2 Timothy 2:22). We should flee all sexual sins in the same way we run from a burning building.

We're also to flee idolatry, which is the worship of anything other than God. Idolatry also includes anything we love more than God. This could be money, a person, or our possessions. We should love God above anything. This also means we should never seek after any god other than the Lord God. This includes consulting mediums, fortune tellers, and astrologers. It also forbids attempting to contact the dead and consulting Ouija boards. We're to have nothing to do with any form of the occult.

We are to take the shield of faith which will quench all the fiery darts of the wicked one. Have faith in God, and know all His promises are true. Paul tells us "Faith comes by hearing, and hearing by the word of God" (Romans 10:17). When we're tempted, if we have faith that all God says in His word is true; we won't fall for the lies of the devil.

The Sword of the Word, or the Bible, is our only offensive weapon against the devil. Jesus used Scripture when He was tempted by Satan. With all three temptations from Satan, Jesus answered with a Scripture. We need to know God's Word and memorize verses so that we will be ready with our Sword when it is needed in battle. That's why it's important to study the Bible daily and mediate upon it day and night. The Scriptures are a living Word, unlike any other. "The Word of God is living and powerful, and sharper than any two-edged sword, piercing even to the division of soul and spirit, and of joints and marrow, and is a discerner of the thoughts and intents of the heart." (Hebrews 4:12).

This armor will help us stand firm whenever we're attacked by any member of the unholy trinity—the flesh, the world, or Satan. When we stand firm against any temptation, we prove to God that we're growing in obedience to Him. "Be sober, be vigilant; because your adversary the devil walks about like a roaring lion, seeking whom he may devour. Resist him, steadfast in the faith, knowing that the same sufferings are experienced by your brotherhood in the world" (1 Peter 5:8–9).

Why do we face temptations? Our lives would be easier if we never had to battle the devil.

When Lucifer was expelled from heaven, God could have immediately thrown him into the lake of fire, which is his final destination. But God still had work for him and his demons on earth. Their assignment is to tempt us to disobey God. Why, you ask, would God permit such a thing? You see, God wants to test our character and commitment to Him. By resisting temptation, we're positioning ourselves for advancement in God's kingdom.

God could have made us robots so that we would always obey Him, but that's not what He wanted. God desires that we obey Him willingly. And the only way God can find out if we're obedient is to test us. He allows us to be tempted. Now God never does the tempting; He leaves that to Satan and his demonic hosts. "Let no one say when he is tempted, 'I am tempted by God'; for God cannot be tempted by evil, nor does He Himself tempt anyone. But each one is tempted when he is drawn away by his own desires and enticed" (James 1:13–14).

Each time we're tempted, God is testing us. He always has control over the temptations we face. An example of this is in the book of Job. Satan had to receive permission from God to test Job. Every trial that Job encountered had the consent of God. It's the same with us. The Scripture tells us that we won't be tempted above what we are able to bear. Satan is limited as to what he can do. Nothing happens to us with out God's knowledge and consent.

God has a plan for every person's life; He desires that we accomplish something important for Him, but until God knows that we can handle it, He won't allow us to complete our assignment. That means every time we're under a satanic attack, God is positioning us for advancement in His kingdom. The only way He can find out if we're ready is to allow us to be tempted.

A temptation is set before us, and then God observes how we handle it. If we pass the test, God gives us something greater to do in His kingdom. If we fail, He knows we're still not ready and cannot handle anything greater in His kingdom. Satan and his demons must celebrate when they see one of God's children defeated and God's plan for his life thwarted.

Not only will we not get promoted, we'll receive pay for what we have done—the consequences of our actions. Even if we repent, God doesn't remove the scars so that we are reminded of what we've done.

Then one day, God allows us to retake the test. The temptation is set before us and we pass! We prove to God that we can handle greater responsibility. This time, it's not demonic spirits that celebrate in the spiritual realm; it's angels around God's throne. So the next time you're under a satanic attack, you really can rejoice. God has positioned you for a greater assignment. He's giving you the opportunity to prove you can handle it. God only promotes people of good character and strong commitment to Him. He will not use a dirty vessel. "If anyone cleanses himself from the latter, he will be a vessel for honor, sanctified and useful for the Master, prepared for every good work" (2 Timothy 2:21).

Every one of us goes through this process in our lives. God wants us to live triumphantly. He has a wonderful plan for each of us. The key to achieving it is to be completely surrendered to God in every area. As we come to

Him in total submission to His will, He can do mighty things through us.

Not only will we be rewarded in this life for overcoming temptation, but there are also rewards in heaven. James tells us, "Blessed is the man who endures temptation; for when he has been approved, he will receive the crown of life which the Lord has promised to those who love Him" (James 1:12).

Binding and Loosening

You might have a particular sin that you have been dealing with for years. It could be any number of temptations, but one thing is certain—you can't seem to gain victory over it no matter how hard you try or how often you pray. This could be caused by generational curses that are passed down from parents to child. Some examples are anger, sexual additions, or alcohol abuse. You might know a family where the father is an alcoholic, and his sons and grandsons follow in his steps. There are many sins that can be passed from one generation to the next. These generational curses cause strongholds in our lives.

Beth Moore describes a satanic stronghold in *Living Free* (page 10) as "anything that exalts itself in our minds, pretending to be bigger or more powerful than our God. It steals our focus and causes us to feel overpowered. Controlled. Mastered."

God has given us a weapon to break these strongholds of the enemy—binding and loosening. I learned a lot about binding and loosening by reading Liberty Savard's book, *Shattering Your Strongholds*. She states that binding and loosening are the keys to victory against Satan and our own old natures. Jesus said, "I will give you the keys of the kingdom of heaven, and whatever you bind on earth will be bound in heaven, and whatever you loose on earth will be loosed in heaven" (Matthew 16:19).

I never understood binding and loosing until I read *Shattering Your Strongholds*. Savard explains that there are two kinds of binding. One is to imprison and chain demonic spirits. She also explains how she binds her will, thought, and life to the will of God. She uses the following illustration to make this point, "At once I began to picture a parent binding a baby to their body with a cloth baby-wrap as was used in the sixties and seventies. When that little one was bound to the parent, wherever the parent went, the baby went."

She gives an example of a prayer we can pray to bind and loose. I have tried this, and I am amazed at the results. I have had more power and victory in my life since I have done so. Here is the prayer she suggest you use:

"Lord, I'm standing on the truth of your Word. You said you would give me the keys to the kingdom, that whatsoever I would bind on earth would be bound in heaven and whatsoever I would loose on earth would be loosed in heaven. Right now, in the name of Jesus, I bind my will to the will of God, that I will be constantly aware of His will and purpose for my life. I bind myself to the truth of God that I will not be deceived by the many subtle deceptions of the world and the devil.

"I bind myself to the blood of Jesus, that I will never take it for granted. I want to be constantly aware of the miracle-working power to restore and heal and keep me safe. I bind myself to the mind of Christ that I will be aware of how Jesus would have me think in every situation I come into this day. I do not want to react out of my own human, carnal thoughts when situations arise suddenly, I want to think and act as Jesus would have me act. I bind my feet to paths of righteousness that my steps will be steady and true all day long. I bind myself to the work of the cross in my life so that I will continue to die daily to my own selfish desires and motivations and be more like Him.

"I bind the strong man so that I may spoil his household and take back every bit of joy, peace, blessing, freedom, and every material and spiritual possession that he has stolen from me. I take them back right now! Satan, I loose your influence over every part of my body, soul, and spirit. I loose, crush, smash and destroy every evil device you may try to bring into my sphere of influence during this day.

"I repent of every wrong desire, attitude and pattern of thinking I have had. Forgive me, Lord, for holding onto wrong ideas, desires, behaviors and habits. I renounce and reject these things. In the name of Jesus Christ, I loose (destroy, crush, break, smash, melt, etc.) every wrong attitude, pattern of thinking, belief, idea, desire, behavior and habit I have ever learned. I loose the strongholds around them that would keep me from being completely surrendered to the will of God for my life. I loose all doubt and confusion from myself.

> "I have bound myself to the mind of Christ and I loose every wrong thought and evil imagination that will keep me from being in sweet unity with Him. I bind and loose these things in the name of Jesus Christ, who has given me the keys to do so. Thank you, Lord, for the truth."

Wow! That is powerful. Since I have been praying this, I have had more victory in my life than ever before. I hope you pray this every day, and share it with your friends. Every Christian should pray this way daily. Satan would have no power over us if we did.

You can also use a similar prayer to pray for your children. Here is the prayer she suggests you pray for them:

> "In the name of Jesus Christ, I bind _____'s body, soul and spirit to the will and purposes of God for his/her life. I bind _____'s mind, will and emotions to the will of God. I bind his/her to the truth and to the blood of Jesus. I bind his/her mind to the mind of Christ, that the very thoughts, feelings and purposes of His heart would be within his/her feelings and purposes of His heart would be within his/her thoughts.
>
> "I bind _____'s feet to the paths of righteousness that his/her steps would be steady and sure. I bind him/her to the work of the cross with all of its mercy, grace, love, forgiveness, and dying to self.
>
> "I loose every old, wrong, ungodly pattern of thinking,

attitude, idea, desire, belief, motivation, habit, and behavior from him/her. I tear down, crush, smash, and destroy every stronghold associated with these things. I loose any stronghold in his/her life that has been justifying and protecting hard feelings against anyone. I loose the strongholds of unforgiveness, fear, and distrust from him/her.

"I loose the power and effects of deceptions and lies from him/her. I loose the confusion and blindness of the god of this world from _____'s mind that has kept him/her from seeing the light of the gospel of Jesus Christ. I call forth every precious word of Scripture that has ever entered into his/her mind and heart that it would rise up in power within him/her.

"In the name of Jesus, I loose the power and effects of any harsh or hard words (word curses) spoken to, about, or by _____. I loose all generational bondages and associated strongholds from _____. I loose all effects and bondages from him/her that may have been caused by mistakes I have made. Father, in the name of Jesus, I crush, smash and destroy generational bondages of any kind from mistakes made at any point between generations. I destroy them right here, right now. They will not bind and curse any more members of this family.

"I bind the strong man, Satan, that I may spoil his house, taking back every material and spiritual possession he has wrongfully taken from _____. I loose the enemy's influences over every part of his/her body, soul, and spirit. I loose the enemy's influences over every part of his/her body, soul, and spirit. I loose, crush, and smash, every evil device he may try to bring into his/her sphere of influence during this day.

"I bind and loose these things in Jesus' name. He has given me the keys and the authority to do so. Thank you, Lord, for the truth. Amen."

Savard suggests that you pray this prayer every day for your children until they are firmly established in the faith. Don't stop when you first see results because the strongholds that Satan has may be retaken until their faith is secure. I pray this prayer daily for my son, that Satan's grip on him would be broken.

Conclusion

This chapter has been valuable to me, and I hope it has been the same for you. May this information help you live triumphantly in very area of your life.

Endnotes

1. J. Dwight Pentecost. Your Adversary the Devil (Grand Rapids, Mi: Kregel Publications, 1997), P. 16.
2. Beth Moore, *Living Free* (Nashville, Tennessee: LifeWay Press, 2001), page 10.
3. Liberty Savard, *Shattering your Strongholds* (Gainesville, Florida: Bridge-Logos Publishers, 2001), pages 131–132, 171–173.

My People Perish for Lack of Knowledge

Vitality—the dictionary defines this as being vigorous and energetic. We all want vitality and a long life, but how do we acquire it? Jesus said, "I have come that they may have life, and that they may have it more abundantly" (John 10:10). The book of Proverbs also tells us that we can have a long life; but like many of God's promises, this one is conditional. "My son, do not forget my law, but let your heart keep my commands; for length of days and long life and peace they will add to you" (Proverbs 3:1–2).

Every human being has a predetermined number of days on earth. None of us will choose when we'll be born or when we'll die. But let's consider the number of days we do have. How can we live them with vitality and good heath? Is obeying God's laws the only key, or are there other factors to consider? Sometimes, even Christians who live consecrated lives still develop serious illnesses.

Since God has promised us a long, abundant life, but many of us aren't experiencing it, we must lack certain truths that prevent us from achieving our goal. The Scripture tells us, "My people are destroyed for lack of knowledge" (Hosea 4:6). What information do we lack that prevents us from living a long, abundant life? In this chapter, we'll explore a number of factors that will help us achieve our goal.

We all make choices every day. Among those are the foods we eat, how we're going to handle our problems, and whether or not to exercise. When we make these decisions, we usually don't think about their long-tern effects. One thing's for certain, every one of these decisions will affect us down the road. Let's see the consequences of some of these actions.

Most of us don't think much about what we eat. We want to consume foods we like. We want fast or processed foods because they require little or no preparation, and they taste good. With our busy life-style, these are a real time-saver. Oh, we know that donuts and French fries aren't good for us, but we eat them any way. We don't consider what the hydrogenated fats and refined sugar do to our body. We just want to eat the foods we like. We lack self-control with our eating habits. Now we generally control our other physical appetites. Most of us don't steal other people's possessions or take someone else's spouse; but when it comes to food, we all make some poor choices. And these choices over a life-time can lead to serious diseases, even death.

We don't see eating junk food or gluttony as sin, but the way we eat causes sickness and destroys our body. We often don't see the connection between what we eat and our illnesses. Then when disease strikes, we wonder why it happened to us. After all, we might be serving God to the best of our ability. We try to keep His commandments. I know a devout Christian woman who developed cancer. She cried out to God, "Why did you let this happen to me?" He seemed to speak into her spirit, "You did it to yourself."

Even the godliest saints can harm their body, often unaware of what they're doing. When we do this, even unintentionally, the consequences can be deadly. Oh, if we only knew the harm we're causing ourselves by what we eat!

Our body is a special gift from God.

> "Do you not know that your body is the temple of the Holy Spirit who is in you, whom you have from God, and you are not your own. For you were bought at a price; therefore glorify God in your body and in your spirit, which are God's."
>
> 1 Corinthians 6:19–20

Our body is not our own. God made it, Christ redeemed it, and the Holy Spirit lives in it. Everything we do with our body should glorify God including the foods we eat.

Food in biblical times was much more wholesome than what we have today. They didn't have hydrogenated fats such as margarine and shortening that clog arteries and cause cancer. They didn't have sugar and refined flour. There was no genetically engineered, pesticide strayed, processed groceries. Their food was pure and wholesome. What they ate didn't come from a box or can; everything was fresh and homemade. Their provisions were wholesome and promoted good health.

If we want to remain healthy, that's how we need to eat. We might not be able to eat exactly as they did in biblical times, but we can eat more nourishing meals. When we restrict our diet to wholesome foods, our body can achieve homeostasis. This is a condition in which all of our systems work the way they were designed to do. When homeostasis is achieved, we don't get diseases. Blood flows freely through our arteries. Free radicals that cause cancer are quickly eliminated. Our immune system attacks bacteria and viruses as they are designed to do. We have vitality because every organ is working properly. We don't get arthritis, diabetes, cancer or any other diseases when we're in homeostasis.

But how do I know which foods to eat, and which not to eat?

The secret is whole foods. We need to eat foods in their most natural state—the way our Creator made them. For example, God gave us beef, not beef hot dogs. He gave us eggs, not Egg Beaters. God made whole grains for bread, not white, bleached flour. When man tampers with food, he takes out ingredients that are vital to good heath. Or he puts in additives that cause us harm. We can choose to eat processed foods created by man, or we can choose wholesome foods created by God. One brings death, the other gives life. If we want a long abundant life, we must choose whole foods that promote life.

There's a connection between whole, holy, and heath. They come from the same root word *Sozo*, meaning salvation, or to be made whole, or in good heath. To be made whole or in good heath, we must eat whole foods. Whole foods make us whole, therefore pleasing God and keep us holy.

What do you mean by whole foods?

Whole foods are in their natural state; they're not processed and refined by man. For example, whole grains, such as whole grain wheat, barley, and rice, have all their natural ingredients. Whole grains are made of three parts—the bran, germ, and endosperm. The bran provides fiber, B vitamins, and some protein. The germ provides oils, vitamins, and some protein. The endosperm gives starch, protein, and some B vitamins. These ingredients are important in keeping the body healthy.

When we eat bread made with white flour, we're robbing our body of the essential ingredients needed to function properly. White flour and white rice has been stripped of the bran and the germ. The fiber and most of the nutritional elements have been taken out. Some vitamins have been put back in, but not all, and none of the fiber is restored. Bread is meant to be an important part of our diet, but bread made from white flour is mostly empty calories with a few vitamins. People who only eat white bread are setting themselves up for major diseases.

There is a benefit of making bread with multiple whole grains. God gave Ezekiel this recipe: "Take for yourself wheat, barley, beans, lentils, millet, and spelt; put them unto one vessel, and make bread of them for yourself" (Ezekiel 4:9). God has the exact recipe for nutritious bread.

It isn't only whole grains that make us whole or healthy. We need whole fruits and vegetables. By whole, I mean the whole fruit or vegetable the way God made them, not canned or over-cooked. Raw fruits and vegetables have all the vitamins and minerals still in them. Frozen foods also retain much of their nutritional value.

A wide variety of fruits and vegetables exists, and no two are exactly alike. We need to eat an assortment of foods to get all the nutrition we need. Fruits and vegetables that are cooked should be heated at low temperature; high temperature destroys most of the nutrition.

Cooking also destroys the enzymes. Enzymes are substances that break down our food so that it can be digested. If there are no raw foods with our meal, the food can't be digested; and it rots in our stomach. The rotten food comes back up our esophagus, causing acid reflux. Every meal should have a serving of raw fruit or vegetables. It does little or no good to eat a wholesome meal with only cooked foods. If you can't eat raw foods with a meal, you can take enzyme tablets. These contain all the enzymes you need to digest your foods. They can be purchased at a health food store.

The Power of Green

Do you want more energy and vitality? Many people depend on coffee to perk them up each morning. They get a quick boost, but later in the day they feel drained. That's because coffee is sprayed with pesticides and has other additives. Each time we drink a cup of coffee, we're filling God's temple with poison.

Before I learned of the harmful affects of coffee, I drank at least one cup each morning, and I savored every drop of it. But later in the day, I felt tired. But I continued to drink coffee because I liked it and it gave me a good start to the day. But I knew I had to stop poisoning myself.

Now I drink a cup of green tea instead. Once I stopped thinking about coffee, I began to enjoy my cup of tea. It helps me wake up without feeling let down later. But that's not all. I haven't had one cold since I've been drinking tea instead of coffee. Green tea also helps regulate blood sugar, aids in burning fat, and boosts the immune system. A word of caution—green tea, as with all teas, lowers the iron level. If you drink green tea, you'll need to increase your iron intake. Do not take an iron supplement without a doctor's supervision.

Green tea isn't the only green that will give you a boost. Green leafy vegetables are a power house of energy. This includes green leaf lettuce, dandelion greens, Swiss chard, spinach, mustard greens, and Romaine lettuce. Why do they give us so much energy? All of these have chlorophyll made from the sun. When we eat green leafy vegetables, we get energy from the sun. These provide more vitality than a cup of coffee and without the harmful side affects. They also provide many vitamins, calcium and other nutrients. These can be eaten raw in salads, or cooked lightly over low heat.

Greens such as kale, mustard greens, and spinach need to be cooked slightly in order to be broken down. They can't be digested when they're eaten raw. These can also be put into a blender and made into a green drink. However you choose to eat them, they taste good and are good for you.

Much of what we eat is dead foods. These are packaged, canned, or refined until all the life has gone out of them. Fresh fruits and vegetables give us life. The green leafy vegetables give us energy and vitality. Instead of filling up on junk foods, why not eat more salads, vegetables and fruit? These are low in calories and they'll provide you with vitality and good health.

The Dietary Laws in the Old Testament—Do They Apply to Us Today?

God gave Moses the dietary laws in the eleventh chapter of Leviticus to keep His people healthy. These laws forbid the eating of certain meat and seafood.

> "Speak to the children of Israel, saying, 'These are the animals which you may eat among all the animals that are on the earth: Among the animals, whatever divides the hoof, having cloven hooves and chewing the cud—that you may eat. Nevertheless these you shall not eat among those that chew the cud or those that have cloven hooves….These you may eat of all that are in the water: whatever in the water has fins and scales, whether in the seas or in the rivers—that you may eat'."
>
> Leviticus 11:2–4,9

Most Christians today don't observe these dietary laws, but should we? Jesus said, "Do not think that I came to destroy the Law or the Prophets. I did not come to destroy but to fulfill" (Matthew 5:17). Jesus' death fulfilled the requirement of blood sacrifices for the sins of the world. We no longer need to offer sacrifices every year as the children of Israel did.

Does that mean that the other laws in the Old Testament should be ignored by Christians? Most of those laws don't apply to us today. But it makes sense to keep the dietary laws. Every one of those unclean animals that God forbids the Jews to eat causes diseases. If they are harmful to the Jews, wouldn't they be harmful to us also?

What about Peter's vision of unclean animals? Didn't God tell Peter that what He cleansed should not be called common?

This refers to Peter receiving Gentiles in his home. He said to Cornelius, "You know how unlawful it is for a Jewish man to keep company with or go to one of another nation. But God has shown me that I should not call any man common or unclean" (Acts 10:28). God wasn't referring to animals. That vision was to instruct Peter that no human being should be called unclean.

Why did God tell His people not to eat certain meats and some kinds of fish? The fish and seafood that God forbids to be eaten are bottom feeders. That means they're garbage collectors. Among these are lobster, shrimp, catfish, clam, crabs, and eel. Every time we eat one of these fish, we're also eating the waste they collect. No wonder God said not to consume them.

Among the animals God forbids us to eat are pork and rabbit. God created all the clean and unclean animals. Since He made every creature, He knows which ones are good for food and which ones cause illnesses. If He forbids certain animals from being eaten, it's for our benefit. If you read the laws God gave Moses in the book of Leviticus, you'll see that each of these were intended to promote the health God's people.

Fats—the Good, and the Bad, and the Very Good

God also forbids the eating of animal fat. "This shall be a perpetual statute throughout your generations in all your dwellings: you shall eat neither fat nor blood" (Leviticus 3:17). There's a good reason that God forbids the eating of animal fats. We now know that this causes heart disease. But are all fats harmful? Some are good, even essential for our health. In fact, the right kinds of fats and oils help us fight degenerative diseases, give us vitality, and improve our brain function. Every cell in our body relies on fats to work properly. In this section, we'll look at both good and bad fats.

Most fats and oils from plants start out as nutritious whole foods, such as corn or canola oil. Then they're heated at such high temperatures that all the life-giving nutrients are destroyed. This process is called hydrogenation. Margarine, shortening, and most cooking oils are hydrogenated. Hydrogenated fats resemble plastic when they're put under a microscope. Our body can't digest these plastic look-alikes because they're not real food; therefore, our body stores them in our cells.

In his book, *Facts about Fats,* John Finnegan describes studies that have shown that trans-fatty acids from refined oils are a major cause of heart disease and cancer. These are the two leading causing of death in America. He contributes this in a large part to refined cooking oils and margarine. Instead of getting essential fatty acids which we need to fight diseases, we're taking in rancid oils that are poisoning us.

What should we use instead?

Cooking oils that are cold pressed retain all their nutrients. Cold pressed refers to heating at temperatures of 118 degrees F or less. Most cooking oils in the supermarket are hydrogenated. Those that are cold pressed will state it on the label. Extra virgin olive oil is cold pressed. (Make sure the label says extra virgin olive oil, not just olive oil or light olive oil.) Cooking oils that are cold pressed provide us needed nutrients such as essential fatty acids and vitamin E.

Butter is another natural substance, and it's much better than margarine which is hydrogenated and contains toxic trans-fatty acids. (Butter can be left out at room temperature except in hot weather.) Butter is a natural substance that your body can properly digest, unlike hydrogenated margarine. Butter contains saturated fat, so use it sparingly.

Because of the fats we use, most of us are deficient in Omega 3 fatty acids. These are essential for fighting cancer, heart disease, and other illnesses. An excellent source of Omega 3 is flax seed oil. It prevents and helps cure cancer, fights heart disease, emotional disorders, improves brain functions, boost energy, and helps fight infections. Unlike other cold pressed oils, it must be refrigerated because its nutrients are easily destroyed. It can't be used in cooking. It's good mixed in salads or cottage cheese, but don't use more than two or three tablespoons per person per day. I add flax seed oil to our food just before it's served. You can purchase flax seed oil at a heath food store.

Other sources of high-quality fats are fish and nuts. If you want to stay healthy, you'll need to include a variety of the right kinds of fats in your diet daily.

Sugar

Do you have an abundance of energy and feel great most of the time? Or are you tired and have a few aches and pains? If you're like most people, you feel sluggish and you probably have some part of your body that hurts.

Most people have no idea that sugar is often the root cause of their discomfort. Sugar and NutraSweet cause many illnesses and even death. Oh, these killers won't harm you immediately, but they will over time. It's our lack of knowledge about sweeteners that kill a lot of people. "My people are destroyed for lack of knowledge" (Hosea 4:6).

What is it about sugar that's so destructive? Sugar has a number of adverse affect on our body. Let's start with the mineral imbalance it causes. Even though we need only a small amount of them, minerals are vital for the proper functioning of your body. Sugar requires a number of minerals in order to be digested. These minerals are present in the sugar cane before it's processed. During the refining, all the minerals are stripped away. Where does your body get the magnesium, chromium, manganese, cobalt, copper, and zinc it needs to digest sugar? It takes them from what you have stored. When your body takes minerals out of storage, it throws your mineral ratio off balance. That's why you feel tired two hours after you eat sugar. When you eat additional sugar throughout the day, your body continues to take them out of storage, eventually leaving you depleted. Even if you eat a healthy meal, but end it with dessert, it does you little or no good. Your mineral ratio has been unbalanced, leaving you vulnerable to disease.

The minerals that your body uses to digest sugar are vital to the functioning of your body's systems. When sugar depletes your mineral supply, you are no longer in homeostasis. This eventually leads to a host of illnesses. Some of these are diabetes, arthritis, cancer, osteoporosis, and heart diseases. Sugar is not the only cause of these diseases, but it is a major factor in these and many others.

I learned a lot about the affects of sugar by reading *Lick the Sugar Habit,* by Nancy Appleton. In her book, she explains how sugar contributes to each of the diseases listed above. She also explains how sugar lowers our immune system, making us more susceptible to colds and infections. It also upsets the calcium and phosphorus ration, causing a calcium deficiency. But that's not all. Sugar also affects the endocrine glands. Appleton states, "Each gland sends hormones into the bloodstream, chemical messengers which determine how the body works. The intake of harmful foods like sugar reduces the efficiency of the glands, causing a smaller secretion or altered composition of hormones. This, in turn, has a detrimental effect on the body chemistry" (Page 17).

We think of sugar in desserts such as ice cream, cakes, and pies; but these aren't the only source of sweeteners. Sometimes it's hidden in foods we don't usually thing of. For example, it's found in spaghetti sauces, many types of bread, most breakfast cereals, numerous packaged foods, and jelly. When we eat these foods, we're taking in additional poisons into our system.

Let's take a look at some sugar alternatives. How about NutraSweet? It claims to be a natural substance, but it isn't. It's made up of three ingredients: aspartic acid, phenylalanine, and methanol. Methanol is a wood poison that affects the brain, optic nerve, and retina. NutraSweet is found in many diet foods and it causes a host of illness. Some of these are: brain tumors, headaches, learning problems, epilepsy, impaired vision, anxiety attacks, blindness, allergic reactions, and seizures. This is only a partial list of illnesses caused by NutraSweet. From what I've read about this product, it's even worst that sugar.

People do much harm to their body by eating sugar and NutraSweet. They have no idea that these sweeteners could be the root cause of their illness. They go to their doctor and get a prescription drug to treat their symptoms. Most doctors are dedicated professionals who have only been taught to give prescriptions to treat diseases. They usually know little about nutrition. They write a prescription. These drugs usually cause side affects, so the patient receives another prescription. People spend a lot of money on medications, doctor bills and hospital stays. If they only knew that most often, their illnesses are caused by what they eat. Hosea was certainly correct when he wrote that "My people perish for lack of knowledge Hosea" 4:6.

Does that mean to be healthy you have to give up all sweets? Not at all! There are some natural sugar substitutes. Raw honey is one. Honey purchased in the grocery store has been refined and depleted of its minerals just as sugar has, but raw honey is unprocessed and is a natural sweetener. Turbinado, which is what is left of the sugar cane when it's processed, is also a natural sweetener. It contains all minerals that were taken out of the sugar cane during refining. Turbinado is courser and darker than refined sugar. Stevia is another natural sweetener. As with all sugar substitutes, use them sparingly. The book of Proverbs tells us, "Have you found honey? Eat only as much as you need. Lest you be filled with it and vomit" (Proverbs 25:16). This is good advice for all natural sweeteners.

When I discovered how harmful sugar is, I stopped eating foods which contain it. The first couple of days without sugar were difficult! I craved the sweetener and I had a headache from not eating it. In three days, the headache and craving were gone, and I had more energy than I had ever had. With in a few days, the bursitis in my left arm went away as well as the arthritis in my fingers. I had no idea that sugar was causing these diseases, as well as draining my energy. Today, I eat sugar only once in a while. I've found that if I eat it every day, I feel tired and the bursitis and arthritis come back.

Several years ago, I taught classes in weight loss and nutrition. In each class, I asked the women to go home and rid their cupboards of every thing that contained sugar, hydrogenated oils, processed foods, and white bread. They ate only whole foods, cut back on their portion sizes, and exercised several times a week. They were amazed at how much better they felt and how much more energy they had. But even more amazing, sometimes their doctors took them of prescription drugs. These were women who had been taking medications for arthritis, high blood pressure, and diabetes. After eating only whole foods, they no longer needed medication. (None of these women stopped taking prescriptions without their doctors' consent.) This demonstrates what happens when we give our body proper nutrition and eliminate sweets and processed food from our diet.

If we insist on committing suicide with a fork, God won't stop us. We have free will to decide which foods we eat, and whether or not to exercise. We can choose to eat the all-American diet of refined foods which bring an assortment of diseases. Or we can discipline ourselves to eat foods that are good for us. That doesn't mean that to be healthy, you can never eat another baloney sandwich or candy bar. It's all right for a healthy person to eat occasionally something they crave as long as the majority of their meals are made from whole foods. What we choose will determine whether we get degenerative diseases and perhaps die prematurely or live a healthy, triumphant life.

Eating junk food isn't the only way to upset our body chemistry. We can also accomplish this by stress and worry. The Psalmist tells us, "Cast your burden on the Lord, and He shall sustain you; He shall never permit the righteous to be moved" (Psalm 55:22). Many illnesses can be traced to stress because we worry about our problems rather than turn them over to the Lord. Elsewhere in this book, we've discussed praising God when we're in a difficult situation. Instead of worrying about our problems, we should turn them over to God, and praise Him in every situation. Stress and worry can cause as much harm to our body as eating junk food.

Fasting

Once you decide to eat only whole foods, you're on your way to living a healthy and triumphant life. If you want to be at your best, there's still something else you need to do. You've spent years accumulating toxins in your body. These come from food additives, medications, and air pollution. Your body also produces toxins as a by-product of cell metabolism. You've been carrying all those poisons around for years, and they're draining your energy. To be at your best, you need to allow your body to clean house.

The only way your body can rid itself of toxins is by fasting. Going without food allows your cells to clean out the debris that's been stored there for years. When your body is constantly digesting food, it can't dispose of the toxins that accumulate in the cells. During the day, our body is busy digesting food. We eat one meal after another, not allowing the cells time to clean house.

Our body does have a few hours of rest during the night. Our cells begin the process of getting rid of pollutants. But in the morning, we break our fast with breakfast. Our body doesn't have time to complete its job. It takes three days of fasting to rid the body of toxins.

In biblical times, fasting was a normal way of life. Jesus said "when you fast," not *if* you fast. He assumed people were already fasting. A healthy person can go without food for three days. To keep up your strength, you can drink water, broth, or pure fruit or vegetable juice during a fast. If you fast for longer than three days, consult with your doctor.

Not every one should fast. Any one with a serious illness, eating disorder, children, pregnant women or nursing mothers, a person who fears fasting, or an emaciated person shouldn't fast without their doctor's permission. Your body lives off stored fat while you fast. A person who doesn't have stored fat will take nourishment from their vital organs if they don't eat. Sometimes, a doctor will give permission for someone in one of these categories to do a partial fast, where they eat only fresh fruits and vegetables and fresh juices. Your body can detoxify when you eat fresh fruits and vegetables because they are easier to digest than cooked foods.

Fasting is also a powerful aid to prayer. Prayer and fasting can do more than prayer alone. Some demonic spirits' power can only be broken by prayer and fasting. Once, Jesus' disciples tried to cast out a demon from a child, but they were unsuccessful. Jesus told them, "This kind does not go out except by prayer and fasting" (Matthew 17:21).

When you fast, you'll have more energy, your eyes will sparkle, and you'll look younger. But that's not the best part. After your body cleans out toxins, it actually begins to heal itself. The body can heal itself of just about any disease, except cancer, by fasting. But this needs to be monitored by a health care professional.

Conclusion

How much God loves you! He created you to do a specific task on the earth. He wants you to live a full, abundant life. And you can if you stay spiritually and physically fit. When you give your body whole foods, exercise several times a week, and limit your stress by giving your problems to the Lord, you can live triumphantly.

A Royal Priesthood, a Chosen Generation

Royalty—what comes to your mind with you think of that word? Do you imagine a king sitting on his throne? Are you aware that if you're a child of God, you too, are royalty? "You are a chosen generation, a royal priesthood, a holy nation, His own special people, that you may proclaim the praises of Him who called you out of darkness into His marvelous light" (1 Peter 2:9).

Your royal status will someday be elevated to co-reign with Christ. You will sit with Him, and rule with Him on His throne. That thought is almost too awesome to comprehend, but it's true. "To him who overcomes I will grant to sit with Me on My throne, as I also overcame and sat down with My Father on His throne" (Revelation 3:21). We will someday actually sit with Christ on His throne and judge the world. "Do you not know that the saints will judge the world?...Do you not know that we shall judge angels?" (1 Corinthians 6:2–3).

Heirs to the British throne spend their childhood preparing to rule their country. From an early age, they are trained how to conduct themselves and how to make decisions. The British monarchy is mostly symbolic now, but the heir apparent still prepares for his role.

If heirs to the British throne spend many years in preparation for their roles, how much more important it is for us to prepare to reign with Christ. The experiences we have here are all intended to work towards that goal. "We know that all things work together for good to those who love God, to those who are the called according to His purpose. For whom He foreknew, He also predestined to be conformed to the image of His Son" (Romans 8:28–29).

God uses the circumstances of our lives to mold us into the image of His Son. He has placed you exactly where you can benefit the most from your experiences. It was no accident that you were born into your family. God chose your parents and place of birth for a reason. Perhaps you didn't have the best parents or the best situation when you were growing up, but God has used those circumstances to shape who you are. You might not be in an ideal situation now, but God is still using your circumstances to grow you up in the image of His Son. Those obstacles are intended to draw you into a closer relationship with Christ and to depend on Him. Every person experiences trials at times in their lives. All the experiences of this life are preparing you for your future role as co-ruler with Christ.

Those trials sometimes include suffering for our faith. Right now, Christians around the world are beaten, imprisoned, and killed because of their belief in Jesus Christ. In this chapter, we'll examine God's purpose in allowing His people to suffer. We'll see how persecution helps us prepare for our future role as co-rulers with Christ. Jesus said that whoever overcomes will sit with Him on His throne. We'll examine what He meant by overcoming. In the next chapter, we'll look at the rewards God has for those who remain faithful to Him.

It shouldn't surprise us that Christians are persecuted; Jesus told us this would happen in the last days.

> "Then they will deliver you up to tribulation and kill you, and you will be hated by all nations for My name's sake. And then many will be offended, will betray one another, and will hate one another. Then many false prophets will rise up and deceive many. And because lawlessness will abound, the love of many will grow cold. But he who endures to the end shall be saved."
>
> Matthew 24:9–13

No Christian looks forward to persecution, but the rewards are great, and they last for all eternity. "If indeed we suffer with Him, that we may also be glorified together. For I consider that the sufferings of this present time are not worthy to be compared with the glory which shall be revealed in us" (Romans 8:17–18). Therefore, the short time of suffering we might experience seems insignificant compared to our rewards in heaven.

Jesus set an example for all who are persecuted unjustly. Paul tells us

> "Let this mind be in you which was also in Christ Jesus, who, being in the form of God, did not consider it robbery to be equal with God, but made Himself of no reputation, taking the form of a bondservant,

and coming in the likeness of men. And being found in appearance as a man, He humbled Himself and became obedient to the point of death, even the death of the cross. Therefore God also has highly exalted Him and given Him the name which is above every name, that at the name of Jesus every knee should bow, of those in heaven, and of those on earth, and of those under the earth."

Philippians 2:5–10

Jesus suffered a horrible death for us. It was His love for us that led Him to the cross.

Jesus died in order that we could have eternal life. In His suffering, He gave us an example to follow. Let's examine what we can learn from Him.

First, He always wanted to obey His Father. He prayed, "O My Father, if it is possible, let this cup pass from Me; nevertheless, not as I will, but as You will" (Matthew 26:39). Jesus knew the suffering He was about to experience, and He accepted it willingly. He was obedient even to the point of death.

Later, as He faced His accusers, He didn't lash out at them. "He was oppressed and He was afflicted, yet He opened not His mouth" (Isaiah 53:7). He remained silent before His accusers. "Who, when He was reviled, did not revile in return; when He suffered, He did not threaten, but committed Himself to Him who judges righteously" (1 Peter 2:23).

Then He prayed for those who persecuted Him. "Father, forgive them, for they do not know what they do" (Luke 23:34). In the Sermon on the Mount, Jesus taught, "You have heard that it was said, 'You shall love your neighbor and hate your enemy.' But I say to you, love your enemies, bless those who curse you, do good to those who hate you, and pray for those who spitefully use you and persecute you, that you may be sons of your Father in heaven" (Matthew 5:43–45).

This is how He prayed for His enemies: "Father, forgive them, for they do not know what they do" (Luke 23:34). Jesus is an example for all those who suffer for their faith. "For what credit is it if, when you are beaten for your faults, you take it patiently? But when you do good and suffer, if you take it patiently, this is commendable before God. For to this you were called, because Christ also suffered for us, leaving us an example, that you should follow His steps" (1 Peter 2:20–21).

Why would God allow His people to be killed? He could prevent Christians from being persecuted.

Yes, God has the power to prevent His people from suffering, but at times, He chooses not to. As we'll discover, there is a purpose for persecution. God's ultimate purpose in allowing us to suffer is that we would be conformed into the likeness of His Son.

Persecution tests our faith to prove that it is genuine. Some Christians attend church merely to make a good impression or to appear religious. That kind of faith will not stand persecution. Anyone can be baptized and join a church. We can't tell who actually has accepted Christ as their Savior. When someone is persecuted for their faith, it is evident to even unbelievers that their faith is genuine.

Peter makes this point clear in his epistle, "In this you greatly rejoice, though now for a little while, if need be, you have been grieved by various trials, that the genuineness of your faith, being much more precious than gold that perishes, though it is tested by fire, may be found to praise, honor, and glory at the revelation of Jesus Christ" (1 Peter 1:6–7).

Persecution also refines us. When metal is burned at a high temperature, the dross, or impurities, are removed. What remains is pure metal. Persecution removes impurities in our lives in the same way fire removes dross. Peter tells us, "Since Christ suffered for us in the flesh, arm yourselves also with the same mind, for he who has suffered in the flesh has ceased from sin, that he no longer should live the rest of his time in the flesh for the lusts of men, but for the will of God" (1 Peter 4:1–2). When we suffer in the flesh, sin is removed; and we shine like gold refined through fire. Suffering removes dross from our lives.

Some people will find it more difficult than others to withstand persecution. This is true of those who remain babes in Christ. They are saved, but they never grow up. When a person doesn't grow in their faith, they are stagnant. They might go to church for years, but they never pray or read their Bible. Their spirit is undernourished from being feed only once a week.

Others are carnal Christians, that is, they live for the flesh. They don't have a deep commitment to Christ. These believers are not walking in the Spirit. That means their lives are controlled by the flesh, not the Holy Spirit. If persecution comes, they will most likely not be able to withstand the trials that will test their faith.

When the immature and the carnal Christians' faith are tested, they have nothing to hold on to. They're like a foolish man who builds his house on the sand. Jesus taught,

> "Whoever hears these sayings of Mine, and does them, I will liken him to a wise man who built his house on the rock: and the rain descended, the floods came, and the winds blew and beat on that house; and it did not fall, for it was founded on the rock. But everyone who hears these sayings of Mine, and does not do them, will be like a foolish man who built his house on the sand: and the rain descended, the floods came, and the winds blew and beat on that house; and it fell. And great was its fall."
>
> Matthew 7:24–27

To withstand persecution, our lives need to be built on the firm foundation of Jesus Christ.

Is there anything we can do to prepare ourselves for such a time?

Jesus told a parable that can help us:

> "The kingdom of heaven shall be likened to ten virgins who took their lamps and went out to meet the bridegroom. Now five of them were wise, and five were foolish. Those who were foolish took their lamps and took no oil with them, but the wise took oil in their vessels with their lamps. But while the bridegroom was delayed, they all slumbered and slept. And at midnight a cry was heard: 'Behold, the bridegroom is coming, go out to meet him!' Then all those virgins arose and trimmed their lamps. And

the foolish said to the wise, 'Give us some of your oil, for our lamps are going out.' But the wise answered, saying, 'No, lest there should not be enough for us and you; but go rather to those who sell, and buy for yourselves.' And while they went to buy, the bridegroom came, and those who were ready went in with him to the wedding and the door was shut. Afterward the other virgins came also, saying, 'Lord, Lord, open to us!' But he answered and said, 'Assuredly, I say to you, I do not know you.' Watch therefore, for you know neither the day nor the hour in which the Son of Man is coming."

Matthew 25:1–13

What a terrible time for those five foolish virgins. When the Bridegroom came, they had no oil in their lamps and they were left out of the wedding feast. In this parable, the ten virgins represent the Church; the oil is the Holy Spirit. Half of the believers ran out of oil, or the Holy Spirit before the Bridegroom came. In other words, they had abandoned their faith. What would cause fifty percent of the church to be depleted of the Holy Spirit? Could it be that when their faith came under fire, they could not withstand the flames?

If we want to keep oil in our lamps, we must prepare now to insure we don't run out. We must buy the oil while it is yet day and not wait until the midnight hour.

How can I make sure there's enough 'oil in my lamp'? I don't want to run out of the Holy Spirit before the Marriage Supper of the Lamb.

To help us stay faithful to Christ, God must be foremost in our lives. Jesus said, "The first of all the commandments is: 'Hear O Israel, the Lord our God, the Lord is one. And you shall love the Lord your God with all your heart, with all your soul, with all your mind, and with all your strength" (Mark 12:29–30).

We must also develop a deeper relationship with God. How do we accomplish this? "The Lord is with you while you are with Him. If you seek Him, He will be found by you; but if you forsake Him, He will forsake you" (2 Chronicles 15:2). How do we seek Him? Draw near to God and He will draw near to you. How do we draw near to Him? "You will seek Me and find Me, when you search for Me with all your heart" (Jeremiah 29:13). Having a deep commitment to Christ will help us remain faithful to Him no matter what comes against us.

Paul and Silas knew about persecution. They were in an inner prison in Philippi, with their feet in stocks. Instead of complaining, though, they prayed and sang praises to God. As a result, an earthquake shook the prison; and all the doors were open. God can still work miracles today when we praise Him.

Rejoice when you face difficulties. Peter tells us,

> "Beloved, do not think it strange concerning the fiery trial which is to try you, as though some strange thing happened to you; but rejoice to the extent that you partake of Christ's sufferings, that when His glory is revealed, you may also be glad with exceeding joy. If you are reproached for the name of Christ, blessed are you, for the Spirit of glory and of God rests upon you. On their part He is blasphemed, but

on your part He is gloried. But let none of you suffer as a murderer, a thief, an evildoer, or as a busybody in other people's matters. Yet if anyone suffers as a Christian, let him not be ashamed, but let him glorify God in this matter...Therefore let those who suffer according to the will of God commit their souls to Him in doing good, as to a faithful Creator."

1 Peter 4:12–16,19

Another way to prepare for persecution is by hiding God's Word in our hearts. Someday, our Bibles might be taken away from us. The only Scripture we will have then is what we have memorized. If you were imprisoned tomorrow for your faith, how much of God's Word would you have with you? If you want to have God's Word with you then, you need to memorize it now. The enemy may take away our freedom, but he can never take away God's Word that we have hidden in our hearts.

Being connected to a church will help you stay strong in the Lord. The writer of Hebrews tells us, "Let us hold fast the confession of our hope without wavering...not forsaking the assembling of ourselves together, as is the manner of some, but exhorting one another, and so much the more as you see the Day approaching" (Hebrews 10:23, 25). We can see the Day approaching now, and we need to draw strength from other Christians.

Imagine yourself in the following situation that actually happened during a worship service:

"We hate you Christians, and we're going to kill every one of you," the gunman said. He and his cohorts had entered a church in Russia wearing hoods, and carrying machine guns which were pointed at the congregation. "We know not all of you believe the nonsense the church teaches. We'll give those of you who aren't actually Christians one minute to leave."

About half of the congregation rushed out the door. When they were gone, the gunmen locked the doors, put down their weapons, and took off their hoods. "We've come to worship with you, but first we wanted to get rid of the hypocrites," one of them said.

If you had been in that service, what would you have done? Would you have denied Christ and run out the door? "If we endure, we shall also reign with Him. If we deny Him, He also will deny us" (2 Timothy 2:12). That's the decision that we might have to face someday. That's the decision thousands of believers are facing right now. Do we save ourselves and be lost for all eternity? "Whoever seeks to save his life will lose it, and whoever loses his life will preserve it" (Luke 17:33).

Paul tells us, "All who desire to live godly in Christ Jesus will suffer persecution" (2 Timothy 3: 12). Jesus said that we should rejoice and be exceeding glad when we're persecuted. "Blessed are you when they revile and persecute you, and say all kinds of evil against you falsely for My sake. Rejoice and be exceedingly glad, for great is your reward in heaven, for so they persecuted the prophets who were before you" (Matthew 5:11–12).

I have heard the testimony of many people who have suffered persecution, and their reaction to it surprised me. Every one of them was glad for the experience. They said it drew them into a closer relationship with Christ in a way they had never experienced. They also felt it was a privilege to suffer for their faith. Persecuted Christians ask us not to pray that the suffering would end, but that they would be able to endure it. They rejoice in that they are worthy to suffer for Christ. One man was in so much pain that he thought he couldn't endure it any longer. Then he saw a vision of Christ on the cross. He knew if Jesus suffered that much for him, he could stand to suffer for Christ.

Another example of this is Watchman Nee, who was a pastor of a large church in Shanghai, China at the time the Communists took over. His fellow believers urged him repeatedly to leave China before the Communists took complete control of the country, but he refused to leave. He said he wouldn't desert his fellow Christians. Nee was eventually captured and imprisoned because he would not join the official church sanctioned by the State, which really is no church at all. In prison, they tried to "reeducate" him. That is, to get him to deny his faith in Christ. But no matter how they tortured him, he stayed faithful to Christ. For over twenty years, the Communists tried to break him, but they could not. He eventually died in prison. Watchman Nee, like thousands of other Christians, proved that their faith in Christ could not be moved.

Paul tells us, "Our light affliction, which is but for a moment, is working for us a far more exceeding and eternal weight of glory" (2 Corinthians 4:17).

We have seen in this chapter the future role God has for us, which is to rule and reign with Christ. In the next chapter, we'll take a look at the rewards for those who will rule and reign with Him.

You Can't Take it With you—Or Can You?

In the first chapter of this book, we saw the fate of those who choose the road that leads to destruction. We witnessed the moment they realized they will spend eternity in everlasting torment. But what happens to those who chose the path to everlasting life? Let's take a look at what awaits them at the judgment seat of Christ.

Come as we enter the throne room of God where this judgment will soon take place. Straight ahead, we see the Father. He is so holy and powerful. And we're so weak and sinful. We tremble in reverence and awe of Him. How unworthy we are to be in His presence! After all, we're sinners standing before Almighty God. But that's not how He sees us. To God, we're without a spot or wrinkle, washed in the blood of the Lamb.

We fix our eyes on the Father as He sits majestically on what looks like a sapphire throne. Surrounding Him are angels who cry "Holy! Holy! Holy!" This scene is just as Ezekiel described:

> "Above the firmament over their heads was the likeness of a throne, in appearance like a sapphire

stone; on the likeness of the throne was a likeness with the appearance of a man high above it. Also from the appearance of His waist and upward I saw, as it were, the color of amber with the appearance of fire all around within it; and from the appearance of His waist and downward I saw, as it were the appearance of fire with brightness all around. Like the appearance of a rainbow in a cloud on a rainy day, so was the appearance of the brightness all around it. This was the appearance of the likeness of the glory of the Lord."

Ezekiel 1:26–28

Wow! God really is a consuming fire.

You look around and notice that some people are absent. Gone are the hypocrites. Gone are the evil doers. Gone are those who denied Christ. Only believers who walked in the Spirit and endured to the end are present, and all their names are recorded in the Lamb's Book of Life.

Our attention is diverted to some activity beside God's throne. Our eyes shift to see Jesus seated at the right hand of the Father. He arises and steps forward. His hair is as white as snow, and His eyes seem as a flaming fire. He walks toward the multitude. Jesus' face is glowing. He smiles and stretches out his arms to greet us. We sense His delight at finally having His Bride by His side. It is with exceedingly great joy that Jesus presents us to the Father.

As Jesus' arms are uplifted, we notice the nail prints in His hands. Our thoughts instantly turn to the cross where He suffered and died to make this moment possible. On the cross, He took the punishment that we deserve. His precious blood paid the price for all our sins. Being reminded of His sacrifice for us intensifies our love for Him. The joy we feel at being in His presence is too much for words. No experience on earth comes close to being as glorious as this moment. We kneel humbly at His feet and worship more fervently than ever before.

Now Jesus steps forward and approaches us individually. Suddenly, He is standing before you. You arise to your feet, and it seems as if no one else is present. He takes your hand, looks you in the eyes; and thanks you specifically for what you did for His kingdom. His voice is the most magnificent sound you have ever heard. Suddenly, as you look in His eyes you're aware of the depth of His great love for you. You knew all along that Jesus loves you, but you had no idea of the depth of that love. You realize that you will forever be in His presence. Never again will you have pain, sorrow, or suffering. You are so overcome with emotion that tears of joy stream down your face. Jesus lingers for a moment and then moves on. As He steps away, you know this moment will be fixed in your memory forever.

As He leaves, you feel saddened for an instant. Then your excitement is renewed as your thoughts turn towards rewards. Finally, you're about to receive the payment for all your work done one earth, for "we must all appear before the judgment seat of Christ, that each one may receive the things done in the body, according to what he has done, whether good or bad" (2 Corinthians 5:10).

This is a day to rejoice and a day to be ashamed, for everything we've done on earth will soon be revealed. God has recorded our every deed—good or bad, great or small.

Everything on earth that was done in secret is about to be known by all. Every act of kindness we did that no one knew about will now be seen, along with those things we wish we had never done. Even our motives will be exposed. Every thought, word, and deed will be laid bare. "Judge nothing before the time, until the Lord comes, who will both bring to light the hidden things of darkness and reveal the counsels of the hearts. Then each one's praise will come from God" (1 Corinthians 4:5).

Every word we've uttered has been recorded—our words of kindness and praise; along with the gossip, complaining, and slander. And those words are about to justify or condemn us. Jesus said, "Every idle word men may speak, they will give account of it in the Day of Judgment. For by your words you will be justified, and by your words you will be condemned" (Matthew 12:36–37). We all gasp for each of us has uttered many words that we're ashamed of. And now we must give an account for every one! We see how important it was to choose our words carefully. If only we had lived our lives in anticipation of this day! How ashamed we are of the gossip and complaining that came from of our lips.

We all are guilty of gossip and slander to some degree, but those saints who have asked God for forgiveness, and learned to control their tongue were made righteous. Bringing every word under submission wasn't easy, but that's what they strived to do. "If anyone does not stumble in word, he is a perfect man, able also to bridle the whole body" (James 3:2). (Perfect in this verse refers to being mature.)

Not only will our words be judged, but our works will be as well. This judgment will not include our sins, for Jesus has forgiven us of all our transgressions. It's our works that will pass through God's communing fire, and He will judge everything we've done fairly. "If you call on the Father, who without partiality judges according to each one's work, conduct yourselves throughout the time of your stay here in fear" (1 Peter 1:17). Those who have been given great ability, resources, or opportunity will be judged more harshly. God will expect more from them for "everyone to whom much is given, from him much will be required" (Luke 12:48). Those who have taught the Bible will be judged more strictly. "My brethren, let not many of you become teachers, knowing that we shall receive a stricter judgment" (James 3:1).

Our works are of two types—what we have done for Christ and all of our other deeds. What we have done in Jesus' name will result in gold, silver, or precious stones. All our other work will produce wood, hay, or straw. Everything will be burned by God's consuming fire to determine which type they are. Paul explains this judgment in 1 Corinthian:

> "If anyone builds on this foundation with gold, silver, precious stones, wood, hay, straw, each one's work will become clear; for the Day will declare it, because it will be revealed by fire; and the fire will test each one's work, of what sort it is. If anyone's work which he has built on it endures, he will receive a reward. If anyone's work is burned, he will suffer loss; but he himself will be saved, yet so as through fire."
>
> 1 Corinthians 3:12–15

As you look around, you see some who hang their heads in

shame for they have brought few good works with them. Some were lazy, and others didn't come to Christ until late in life; a few even on their death beds. They're sorry they wasted so much time on earth. How they regret that they focused their attention on acquiring stuff that will burn up. What a waste! If only they had lived their life in anticipation of this day.

Suddenly, they see the purpose for which they were created. They now know the plan God had for their lives for "We are His workmanship, created in Christ Jesus for good works, which God prepared beforehand that we should walk in them" (Ephesians 2:10). They're aware of what the Holy Spirit could have accomplished through them, and they missed it. They missed the success and the joy of achieving something superb for the kingdom of God. They could have helped many people, and in the process, they would have laid up for themselves treasures in heaven.

How could that happen? How could they miss something so important? They realize they were more concerned about the things of the world rather than the kingdom of God. They focused their attention on acquiring more stuff or making an impressing on others. Now all their possessions are burned; and they have few, if any, treasures in heaven.

Some now understand that they couldn't accomplish the task given them because they weren't spiritually ready. God allowed them to go through trials or temptations to test them. He wanted them to prove that they were mature enough to handle more responsibility. But they failed the test. They didn't rely on instructions given in the Bible. Instead, they gave in to the enticement. Or perhaps they grumbled and complained about their trial rather than give it to the Lord. Whatever the ordeal, they proved that they weren't yet ready to handle greater responsibility. Throughout their lives, God gave them additional trials to prove that they were ready for advancement, but each time they failed to follow instructions in the Bible. As a result, they weren't able to complete, or perhaps even begin, the task God had intended for them. Oh, if only they could live again!

They watch regretfully as those who used their talents seem confident and joyful; even though they, too, have wasted hours during their life-time. Even so, much of their work will result in gold, silver, and precious stone. They have quietly done much good in the kingdom of God, which at the time seemed to go unnoticed or unrecognized. Now they are about to receive their reward. They have preached the gospel, directed the choir, taught Sunday school or accomplished whatever plan God had for their lives. The work they did was done for Christ, not to impress others. "Whatever you do, do it heartily, as to the Lord and not to men, knowing that from the Lord you will receive the reward of the inheritance; for you serve the Lord Christ" (Colossians 3:23–24).

After our rewards are distributed, a number of saints who were once considered poor are now rich in gold, silver and precious stones. But many who during their life-time possessed much wealth have only wood, hay, and straw. Others who were wealthy on earth also have riches in heaven. Everyone has exactly the rewards they have earned. No matter how much anyone desires additional rewards, they can't gain more, and no one can ever lose the rewards they have.

Our treasures also include crowns. These are incorruptible, and we'll have them for all eternity. Paul explains our crowns in 1 Corinthians:

> "Do you not know that those who run a race all run, but one receives a prize? Run in such a way that you may obtain it. And everyone who competes for the prize is temperate in all things. Now they do it to obtain a perishable crown, but we for an imperishable crown. Therefore I run thus: not with uncertainty. Thus I fight: not as one who beats the air. But I discipline my body and bring it into subjection, lest, when I have preached to others, I myself should become disqualified."
>
> 1 Corinthians 9:24–27

Let's take a look at the crowns we can receive:

Everyone who eagerly awaited Jesus' return receives a crown of righteousness. Many receive this crown because they eagerly waited His return. "There is laid up for me the crown of righteousness, which the Lord, the righteous Judge, will give to me on that Day, and not to me only but also to all who have loved His appearing" (2 Timothy 4:8).

All who endure testing will receive the crown of life. "Blessed is the man who endures temptation; for when he has been approved, he will receive the crown of life which the Lord has promised to those who love Him" (James 1:12). Temptation in this verse means to endure trials.

Pastors receive the crown of glory.

> "Shepherd the flock of God which is among you, serving as overseers, not by compulsion but willingly, not for dishonest gain but eagerly; nor as being lords over those entrusted to you, but being examples to the flock; and when the Chief Shepherd appears, you will receive the crown of glory that does not fade away."
>
> 1 Peter 5:2–4

Only those pastors who remain faithful to their calling throughout their ministry receive this crown.

Those who led others to faith in Christ receive a crown of rejoicing. "What is our hope, or joy, or crown of rejoicing? Is it not even you in the presence of our Lord Jesus Christ at His coming? For you are our glory and joy" (1 Thessalonians 2:19–20). In this verse, Paul is speaking of those that he had led to the Lord.

Relatively few receive this crown because not many were soul winners, but all who were will shine like the stars forever. "Those who are wise shall shine like the brightness of the firmament, and those who turn many to righteousness like the stars forever and ever" (Daniel 12:3). Both those who initially speak to someone about Christ and those who actually lead them to faith will reap a reward. "He who plants and he who waters are one, and each one will receive his own reward according to his own labor" (1 Corinthians 3:8).

Just when we thought Jesus was finished distributing rewards, we find He has additional ones to give. These are for those who remained faithful to Him through persecution. Jesus said, "Blessed are you when they revile and persecute you, and say all kinds of evil against you falsely for My sake. Rejoice and be exceedingly glad, for great is your reward in heaven" (Matthew 5:11–12). How these saints suffered! They were beaten, tortured, or killed but they would not deny Him. They conquered just as Jesus conquered. "They overcame him by the blood of the Lamb and by the word of their testimony, and they did not love their lives to the death" (Revelation 12:11).

Now their suffering has turned to eternal joy. Paul tells us, "Our light affliction, which is but for a moment, is working for us a far more exceeding and eternal weight of glory" (2 Corinthians 4:17). These are the rewards they will receive:

> "To him who overcomes I will give to eat from the tree of life, which is in the midst of the Paradise of God."
>
> Revelation 2:7

> "Be faithful until death, and I will give you the crown of life."
>
> Revelation 2:10

> "To him who overcomes I will give some of the hidden manna to eat, and I will give him a white stone, and on the stone a new name written which no one knows except him who receives it."
>
> Revelation 2:17

> "He who overcomes, and keeps My works until the end, to him I will give power over the nations—He shall rule them with a rod of iron; They shall be dashed to pieces like the potter's vessels—as I also have received from My Father; and I will give him the morning star."
>
> Revelation 2:26–29

> "He who overcomes shall be clothed in white garments, and I will not blot out his name from the Book of Life; but I will confess his name before my Father and before His angels."
>
> Revelation 3:5

> "He who overcomes, I will make him a pillar in the temple of My God, and he shall go out no more. I will write on him the name of My God and the name of the city of My God, the New Jerusalem, which comes down out of heaven from My God. And I will write on him My new name."
>
> Revelation 3:12

> "To him who overcomes I will grant to sit with Me on My throne, as I also overcome and sat down with My Father on His throne."
>
> Revelation 3:21

Suddenly we notice we've wearing a beautiful white linen garment. It's made from our righteous acts done on earth. All the sacrifices we made, all the work we did for the Lord, all the people we helped, has been woven together to create a garment that will last for eternity. "To her it was granted to be arrayed in fine linen, clean and bright, for the linen is the righteous acts of the saints" (Revelation 19:8). The Bride of Christ is now without a spot or wrinkle, dressed for her wedding day.

Come; enter the Marriage Supper of the Lamb. The Bridegroom himself bids you come. Blessed are all who enter. This is the culminating event of history. The world, and everything in it, was created for this very moment. The King of the Universe is being wed to His eternal bride. And the marriage supper is about to take place. Millions of years have gone into the preparation of this day. What a grand celebration it will be! Many desire to attend, but only those whose names are written in the Lamb's Book of Life are admitted. The invitation went out to all mankind, but relatively few accepted. They will sit with Christ on His throne and rule the world. All the riches of God's glory will be theirs for eternity.

See the Bridegroom at the door. He's waiting for you to enter. There's a seat at the King's table just for you.